D1563111

CHARM
The Elusive Enchantment

JOSEPH EPSTEIN

Guilford, Connecticut

An imprint of The Rowman & Littlefield Publishing Group, Inc.
4501 Forbes Blvd., Ste. 200
Lanham, MD 20706
www.rowman.com

Distributed by NATIONAL BOOK NETWORK

British Library Cataloguing in Publication Information available

Library of Congress Cataloging-in-Publication Data available

ISBN 978-1-4930-3579-3 (hardcover)
ISBN 978-1-4930-3580-9 (e-book)

∞™ The paper used in this publication meets the minimum requirements of American National Standard for Information Sciences—Permanence of Paper for Printed Library Materials, ANSI/NISO Z39.48-1992.

Printed in the United States of America

For Georges Borchardt,
a charmer on two continents

"Subtlety, discretion, restraint, finesse, charm, elegance, good manners, talent, and glamour still enchant me."

—NOËL COWARD
THE NOËL COWARD DIARIES

"It is absurd to divide people into good and bad. People are either charming or tedious."

—OSCAR WILDE
LADY WINDERMERE'S FAN

CONTENTS

INTRODUCTION

THINGS CAN BE CHARMING, AND ANIMALS OFTEN SEEM SO, BUT THE QUESTION of charm is most interesting in connection with human beings. Is human charm a gift from God—or, if one prefers, from the gods, or of the luck of the draw—or is it a talent that requires development and cultivation? How does it function? Does it have a purpose? Might it be overdone? Can we live without it? Who needs it? Is it among the virtues; and if a virtue it be, is it a trivial or a serious one? Who has had charm? Who among us has it today? Is charm now in notably short supply? And if it is—to ask the question is to assume it is—why and how did this come about?

One can of course be charmed by landscapes, buildings, artworks, and so much more. I have myself in recent weeks been driving round the city of Chicago listening to songs written and sung by Johnny Mercer— "I'm Old-Fashioned," "Moon River," "Satin Doll," "Summer Wind," and others—and find myself uplifted by them in the way that only uncomplicated music can raise one's spirits. I never pass Frank Lloyd Wright's Roby House on the University of Chicago campus without feeling elevated by its graceful lines; the same applies to the skyscraper known as the Hancock Building on Michigan Avenue. Merely coasting along the city's Outer Drive, the always changing waters of Lake Michigan to the east, also charms. The darkly comic poems of Philip Larkin and the novels of P. G. Wodehouse unfailingly charm me. For those with an eye for it, charm can be found in many places, but in this book I concentrate on charm in its human aspect, charm as conveyed by human presence, if only to delimit somewhat an already broad and sufficiently complex subject.

Neither do I take up the matter of charm in non-Western cultures: in China, India, Africa, and elsewhere. The only thing vaster than this aspect of the subject, non-Western charm, is my ignorance of it, and for this sound reason I have not taken it up. Besides, as an immensely charming writer named Max Beerbohm said in one of his essays about the need to take up a history of the 1880s, to give an accurate account of so complex a subject "would need a far less brilliant pen than mine."

Almost everyone will recognize when he or she is in the presence of charm. Charm is magic of a kind; it casts a spell. In the presence of charm, the world seems lighter and lovelier. A charming person can cause you to forget your problems and, at least temporarily, to hold the world's dreariness at bay. Charm is a reminder that the world is filled with jolly prospects and delightful possibilities.

Charm is a form of pleasure. One is charmed by another person's looks or personality or general artfulness of presentation. The spell that charm casts takes one out of oneself, lifting one into another, more exalted realm. Watching Fred Astaire dance, or listening to Blossom Dearie sing, or reading the poems of C. P. Cavafy, or merely looking at Rita Hayworth or Ava Gardner, one recalls that the world can be a pretty damn fine place. To be charmed is sometimes to be swept up, blown away, enraptured; at others, to be quietly satisfied, left calmly contented.

Tastes in charm differ vastly. Some are charmed by the merely cute; for others only the exquisite charms. The Three Stooges do it for some, the drawings of Albrecht Dürer for others. A lucky few are charmed by both and much else in between. Ask a person what charms him and you will learn a fair amount about him.

Charm needs to be distinguished from ecstasy and other, higher-powered conditions and states. In the famous distinction between the Apollonian and the Dionysian, based on the reputed interests of the gods Apollo and Dionysus, the Apollonian is bright, lucid, reasonable, ordered, while the Dionysian is ecstatic, intoxicated, chaotic, reaching for the sub-lime, bringing on the fires and dancing girls. The Apollonian seeks the light, the Dionysian thrives in the dark. Alexander Pope, Reynaldo Hahn, Paul Valery, the draughtsman Sempré are Apollonian; Wagner, Baudelaire, Samuel Beckett, Lucian Freud are Dionysian. Charm tends overwhelm-ingly to be Apollonian.

That charm seeks the light does not mean that charm itself needs to be light, or, as we should now say, lite. Charm is calm, rarely agitated;

cool, almost never hot. Charm is graciousness in action; it is never going too far, pushing too hard, staying too long. Some charm is natural, some artificial, though the two categories are not always as distinct as one might imagine. "I am," said Maurice Ravel, composer of some of the world's most charming music, "naturally artificial." And so he was, and in him it worked, charmingly.

Charm is elegance made to seem casual. Charm comes across as at ease in the world. It is virtuosity of personality. Charm is a performance art; behind it is the deliberate decision to be pleasing to others, or, in some cases perhaps, to a selected few. Charm is, or at least often can be, a gift, one that its possessors bestow on others.

Asked to define charm, most people are unable to do so. As I begin to write this book, I am myself less than certain how to define charm. Some might say it is suavity, a kind of confident elegance, and suavity can sometimes be charming, but charm is larger than mere suavity. Others, overestimating charm, say that it is personal charisma. But charisma is much greater than charm; it operates in a much larger arena than charm, while charm tends to operate on a more personal level.

The definition of charm, as with the definitions of all magical things, is elusive. Some people confuse charm with simple courtesy, generosity, thoughtfulness. (A person can be immensely likeable without being especially charming.) All these things are good in and of themselves, but they do not constitute charm. Charm has an element of delight beyond mere niceness. Charm can even be dangerous, as in the case of charming seducers, frauds, and tyrannical politicians, men and women who use charm to maneuver, to manipulate people.

The *Oxford English Dictionary* defines charm as "the power to give delight, or arouse admiration." If a motive behind charm is needed, perhaps it can be established by slightly tweaking the *OED* definition to read "the power to give delight in order to arouse admiration." "He turned on the charm," we say. "His charm escapes me," we also say. Some, of course, might say it about the very same person. For charm is in the eye of the beholder, and the saddest thing, the gravest error in the social realm, is to overestimate one's own charm, a serious faux pas all would-be charmers are in danger of committing.

What charms? Wit, for one thing; gentle humor, for another. So, too, can unmotivated kindness and large-hearted generosity charm. Beauty in the form of good, or even interesting, looks; sometimes striking oddity charms as the French, in deriving the phrase *belle laide*, meaning beautiful-ugly, understood. Eccentricity can charm. Even shyness can charm.

Charm comes in many varieties. Marcello Mastroianni mastered several of them. He could do charming elegance, charming comic, world-weary charming, even slightly seedy charming. Mastroianni is a reminder that charm also comes in national styles: Italian, French, English. American charm can seem more a problem, German charm perhaps even more so. Irish charm is famous, but not everyone's dish of tea. No Irishman, it has been said, is ever charmed by Irish charm. During certain historical periods—the courts of the Renaissance, life at Louis XIV's Versailles—charm had prescribed forms. Charm has always been with us, sometimes in more abundance than others, but perhaps for the first time in its lengthy and complex history, few people today are able to agree on who is charming or even on what constitutes charm.

I had better say straightaway that this book will not teach its readers how to be charming, though it does offer bits of scattered advice about how to avoid being boring and booring—that is to say, distinctly uncharming. Charm is too complex, too many-faceted, too richly various to permit the simple check-list or ten-step formulations preferred by How-To books. Those who have had charm—Lord Byron, say, or Groucho Marx—are too disparate to be locked into the same small definitional box out of which a formula for achieving charm may be expected to spring.

I thought to write a book about charm because my own thoughts on the subject were blurry and I wished to set them out to get them into sharper focus. ("How do I know what I think until I see what I say," wrote E. M. Forster in what as a writer has long been my motto.) I hoped, if I were able to do so, to provide a similar service for anyone who might have a kindred interest and equally inchoate thoughts on the subject. *Charm* is, after all, a word everyone uses, but most people understand in a vague way. Over the years I have written at book length on Ambition, Snobbery, Envy, Friendship, Gossip, and other loosely defined matters that have fascinated me and, I hoped, would fascinate others. "I write for myself and strangers," Gertrude Stein said. I do the same, though I hope more clearly than Miss Stein, with the implicit understanding that these strangers are not so different in their interests, confusions, and temperament than I.

What, then, is charm? Who has it or has had it? Why do we need it? These are the questions this book of modest length immodestly sets out to answer.

PART ONE

CHAPTER I

The Movies Define Charm

EARLY IN HIS NICOMACHEAN *ETHICS*, ARISTOTLE NOTES THAT "OUR DISCUS-
sion will be adequate if it has as much clearness as the subject-matter
admits of; for precision is not to be sought for alike in all discussions, any
more than in all the products of the crafts." Later in the same paragraph
Aristotle adds: "It is the mark of an educated man to look for precision
in each class of things just so far as the nature of the subject admits; it is
evidently equally foolish to accept probable reasoning from a mathemati-
cian and to demand from a rhetorician demonstrative proofs." So, too, we
must "not look for precision in all things alike, but in each class of things
such precision as accords with the subject matter." Charm, such is its elusive nature, may well be one of those subjects about which much can be
elucidated, much adduced by example, but that ultimately eludes absolute
precision of definition. Like goodness, happiness, and love—three other
such grand subjects—charm manages to carry on quite nicely without
the aid of a locked-in, ironclad definition, and so I shall do without such
a definition in the pages that follow.

The notion of charm is in its origin tied to amulets and incantations
that were thought to cast spells or to bring good fortune. Charm brace-
lets, lucky charms, the third time's a charm, he turned on the charm, she
charmed the pants off me, as all these artifacts and idioms attest, charm
was thought to be something mysterious, if not ultimately magical. And so,
even its human form, it may seem to be touched by magic.

The power of charm is still considered something of a mystery. What,
exactly, is it? Charm implies the ability to make others be pleased by,

if not love or adore, those in possession of it. Charm is an aura, which sounds vague, but it can be specific enough in its seductive power. In the presence of charm, we are put into a state of fascination, a mixture of pleasure and admiration, often with a slight but usually not disqualifying touch of envy.

The general effect of charm is to make the world seem a brighter, grander, lovelier, more amusing, yes charming place. Charm drains life of its monotony, drabness, darkness. Charm is a fine antidepressant, short-lived though its duration may be; it lasts, alas, only as long as its purveyor, the charmer, remains in the room, or on the stage or screen or on a recording one is listening to. One doesn't think of charm as profound, though it can be acute, penetrating, and very smart. Charm is tact to the highest power: dedicated to pleasing those on whom it is applied. The first intention of charm is to make people happy, however briefly.

Charm and style are sometimes confused. Charm differs from style in being lighter, less ingrained, more determined to please. One can, after all, have an aggressive, or a rebarbative style. The definitions of style are mani-fold, including among them the various period styles: classical, renaissance, baroque, and so on. Ironic style, ornamental style, straight style are but a few of the other categories. The best definition of style I know is that of "a way of looking at the world." In this definition, style derives from a person's experience and how he has come to understand it and incorpo-rate it into his personality. *Le style c'est l'homme même,* the style is the man, wrote the eighteenth-century scientist Buffon. Charm in this sense isn't so intricately the man or woman who purveys it as is style.

Charm can be learned, perhaps even imitated; style is acquired through experience. Style determines how one reacts to the world, and subse-quently how one acts in it. Some styles are much more winning than oth-ers, richer, grander, more interesting, and to the extent that they are so, are more likely to contribute to a person's charm. But, even though some styles are charming and some charm stylish, charm and style remain distinct.

Many people when asked to define charm bring up the single word *charisma.* Ask people who haven't thought much about what charm is, and a surprisingly large number answer that it is "a certain charisma." They have themselves, I believe, been not so much charmed as mesmerized by a word with a sonorous sound that through sloppy usage long ago lost its original and true meaning. As Virginia Woolf once said about such words, they do not absorb much truth. As defined by the great German sociologist Max Weber, charm meant authority "resting on devotion to the exceptional sanctity, heroism or exemplary character of an individual person, and of the normative patterns or order revealed or ordained by him." Charisma defined leadership and domination on the world stage. Jesus Christ had charisma; so, at the other extreme, had Hitler. Napoleon had charisma, Gandhi had charisma; Charlie Chaplin and Buster Keaton and Myrna Loy had charm but no charisma whatsoever.

Over time, the meaning of the word *charisma* devolved and descended, so that Marilyn Monroe or Lady Gaga is commonly described as having charisma. An actress in a television series about vampires is named Charisma (Carpenter). Avon still has on the market a perfume called Charisma. Such is the fate of sonorous-sounding words in our time; they go from defining the quality of leadership in Jesus to becoming the name of a perfume. No movie star is likely to have charisma, and neither, sad to report, is Tyler, your nine-year-old child.

Nor is charm cool. Cool tends to be detached, distant; charm is social, often warm, suggesting, sometimes actually seeking greater intimacy. One can be cool yet less than likable. Miles Davis was cool, so too were John Coltrane and Charlie Parker, but their coolness was there, like a barbed-wire electric fence, to keep others at a distance. Cool doesn't crave approval. Louis Armstrong and Duke Ellington were more charming than cool. They wished to please. The genuinely cool person may well seek admiration, but gaining approval is not his or her first order of business.

Charm is not style, not necessarily cool, certainly not charisma. What, then, is it? Perhaps the first thing to be said about it is that it is elusive, evading careful definition. Charm is able to do so because it is so multifaceted, not to say multifaced. "Though defining be thought the proper way to make known the proper signification," wrote John Locke, "yet there are some words that will not be defined." Might *charm* be one of those words? "It is no more possible to convey in writing the constituents of a man's charm," wrote S. N. Behrman in *People in a Diary,* "than it is to convey in writing the effects of music." Is this, too, so?

Raymond Chandler described charm as "a kind of subdued magic, controlled and exquisite, the sort of thing you get from good string quartets." Chandler was writing here about the prose of F. Scott Fitzgerald, who could be so charming on the page and often so uncharming in his life. Even though one would like to think otherwise, perhaps no one is wholly charming, or charming full-time, and the best in this realm one can hope for is partial charm. For this reason, at least in the modern era, so many of the models we have for charm come from the movies, where life's rich complexities have never been the first order of business. In the movies Irene Dunne was charming, and so were Jean Arthur and Myrna Loy. In a radically different way, Mae West qualified as charming. The Hepburns, Katherine and Audrey, surely made the cut, the first for her aristocratic brashness, the second for her refinement and elegance. Barbara Stanwyck's ebullience radiated charm.

Male movie stars exhibit not necessarily more but a wider range of charm: from the suavity of Cary Grant in *North by Northwest* to the taciturnity of Gary Cooper in *Love in the Afternoon* to the hilarity of Donald O'Connor in *Singing in the Rain* to the virile charm of James Garner in just about everything. Fred Astaire provided a charm that was largely physical, and all the more astonishing for the fact that, physically, he was far from prepossessing; the way he moved and spoke and dressed made him charming. Laurel and Hardy, and particularly Stan Laurel, could be charming, and of course Charlie Chaplin was about nothing but charm: If you aren't charmed by Chaplin's dance of the bread rolls in *Gold Rush,* intensive psychotherapy is indicated.

If one wants to take the shortest of short courses in charm, one cannot do better than watch the Thin Man movies with William Powell and Myrna Loy, where two charming people play off each other to maximum charming effect. The story is always the same. Powell and Loy are Mr. and Mrs. Nick Charles; he is a former detective, she an heiress; and together they live in plush and (in his case) boozy comfort on her money. He drinks all day and she wears beautiful clothes at night. Although in some of the later movies they have a child (played by Dean Stockwell), in the earlier ones their only dependent is the wire-haired terrier named Asta, himself damned charming.

William Powell has rather a weak chin, not especially good teeth, and he doesn't move all that smoothly. The charm, you might say, is in his accoutrements. He is always elegantly turned out, in beautifully tailored suits and splendid rain- and overcoats; his pajamas and dressing gowns aren't bad, either. Cocktails, delicately mixed and carefully shaken and imbibed at all hours, are his great passion. When a secondary character in one of the Thin Man movies turns down an early morning drink, Powell replies, "That's a mistake."

So charming is William Powell in these movies that some of the crooks he sent to prison, upon their return, don't hold his foiling them against him. He has an antipathy to his own talent for sleuthing, and Myrna Loy, hungering for a little action, is always encouraging him to take up the latest murder case that conveniently lands at the door of their beautifully appointed apartments in plush hotels where efficient room service is available round the clock. "Oh, Nicky," she says, "why not take the case? You are so good at it, darling."

They play their marriage, like nearly everything else in these movies, for laughs and charm. They sleep in single beds, as the Hollywood censorship codes of the day required, but they rarely get much sleep, and are regularly disturbed at all hours by various mugs and thugs knocking on their door seeking Nick's help and resulting in his taking on another case. All this, though furnishing the action for their movies, is viewed as so much distraction by Powell, who wishes only to get back to his drinking. Besides, detection isn't really what the Thin Man movies are about; charm is.

In many of his movies, Cary Grant does William Powell with good looks—not to speak of the world's most perfect perennial tan—and a British accent added. If Powell was pure charm, Grant's was a more mixed proposition. Did women, watching him in his various movies, fantasize making love with him? Grant was sexy in a way that Powell never was. Is sex a part of charm, or something distinct from it? In some of her movies, Marilyn Monroe could be charming, yet no one was sexier, or at least thought sexier, than she. Sexy can be charming chiefly if it is played for laughs. Sexy played steamily, bordering onto the pornographic, is in another category. In *The Seven-Year Itch*, Marilyn Monroe reports to her downstairs neighbor Tom Ewell, who invites her for a drink, that she'll be right down as soon as she takes her underwear out of the refrigerator; on hot nights, she tells him, all disarmingly, she prefers cool underwear. Now that is sexy but also a joke of sorts on sex, and as such charming.

Sexy can be charming, but charming is not necessarily or even usually sexy. In its purest form, charm is devoid of sexiness. One is charming not to seduce but for charm's own sweet sake. Certainly, good looks can be charming, in and of themselves, and so, too, can interesting, even odd, looks. Fred Astaire, who rarely kissed his leading ladies on camera, is a case in point: a smallish man with a large head, big ears, a too-wide forehead, wearing a toupee—and yet taken all together, somehow, immensely charming.

Many are the stories of female actresses who, self-conscious of what they deem a defect in their looks, have plastic surgery and lose their charm. The actress Jennifer Grey, who was lovely in *Ferris Beuller's Day Off* and *Dirty Dancing,* had rhinoplasty and lost the charming look of vulnerability that her less-than-perfect nose lent her, and she seems to have worked very little in movies afterward. Face-lifts, false or capped teeth, and other cosmetic changes, all meant to improve beauty, can divest a face of its natural charm.

Charm can also be homely, if homely in an unmenacing way. Consider the long bland face of Stan Laurel, with the thatch of standing hair atop it. The Marx Brothers, no great beauties to begin with, made themselves homlier even than nature had intended through makeup and odd costumes. Buster Keaton's wide-eyed innocence radiated charm. Ed Wynn's face fluttered with it. Even W. C. Field's red nose—distinctly not acquired through regular participation in winter sports—had its odd charm.

Most of us have encountered charm among friends and acquaintances. Some of us may have had charming parents, or a charming aunt or uncle or cousin, but most people's first encounter with charm was on the movie screen. Without Hollywood movies, few among us are likely to have clear, if any, notions of charm: of what constitutes it, how it works, and above all, what it looks like. For those among us who in their childhoods in the 1940s, '50s, '60s, and '70s went to the movies regularly, Hollywood provided an education as strong, possibly stronger, than any on offer in the classroom. Without the movies, who would have known how to kiss a member of the opposite sex, smoke a cigarette (when smoking was still considered a cosmopolitan and not an antisocial, possibly a suicidal, act), deal with a head waiter, attempt sophisticated conversation, or wear elegant clothes? About urbanity, suavity, worldliness, and other components of charm the movies clued us in.

Today if one asks anyone for a model of charm, he or she is likely to come up first with a movie star, usually not a contemporary one. Cary Grant, Deborah Kerr, Fred Astaire, Myrna Loy are on the list of usual charming suspects. The names of a rich strain of English film actors—Ronald Colman, Douglas Fairbanks Jr., Errol Flynn, James Mason, David Niven, Herbert Marshall, Alec Guinness, Peter Sellers, and up to but not quite including Michael Caine, Albert Finney, and Dirk Bogarde—also come up. In France the great charmers were Jean-Pierre Aumont, Maurice Chevalier, Alain Delon, Jean-Paul Belmondo, and Louis Jourdan. Italy provided Vittorio De Sica, Marcello Mastroianni; Germany, Maximilian Schell and Oskar Werner.

Where did Hollywood get its notions of charm? Some of its directors—Ernst Lubitsch, Leo McCarey, Preston Sturges, Billy Wilder, George Cukor—esteemed charm, and recognized the value of reproducing it for a mass audience. Romantic comedies, in which these men specialized, were often little more than exhibitions of charm in action. Some of these men were themselves charming. (Billy Wilder, whose charm was of the coarse Viennese kind, once claimed that Oscars and other prizes were rather like hemorrhoids, elucidating the remark by adding: "Every asshole has one.") The success of the movies these men made reverberated, and other, often lesser directors began to aim for charm in their movies. Charm, along with gangsters and cowboys, is one of the things the movies do best, or at least once did best.

The movies produced charm in a buffet of types. Among male actors on offer these included the charm of the ultra-masculine Clark Gable, the roguish Errol Flynn, the sensitive Montgomery Clift, the craggy Humphrey Bogart, the gawky James Stewart, the insouciant William Powell; the dazzlingly good-looking Tyrone Power, the sweet Laurel & Hardy, the chaotic Marx Brothers, the innocent Buster Keaton, and many more. Among women there was the charm of the refined Deborah Kerr, the neurotically energized Rosalind Russell, the peppy Ginger Rogers, the spunky Barbara Stanwyck, the wholesome Jeannie Crain, the sophisticated Irene Dunne, the elegant Olivia de Haviland, the beautiful Rita Hayworth, the silken Lauren Bacall, and many more. The movies offered a velvet-lined sample case of charm.

Whether all these actors were charming in life we shall never know. Many, we have come to know, were not. Since their deaths, stories have begun to leak out about the foibles of many of them: the alcoholism of this one, the dullness of that, the sexual predatoriness of another, the reactionary or communist politics of still others. While they were alive, none of this was public knowledge. The powerful Hollywood studios for which they worked understood that these actors were their most valuable property, and as such they protected them, even from themselves, by not allowing any but their well-varnished selves to be on display.

The two main Hollywood gossip columnists, Hedda Hopper and Louella Parsons, were hostage to the great studios, who fed them a careful diet of what they, the studios, wanted the world to know. The questions asked of movie stars in radio interviews were not so much softballs as cream puffs. Talk shows had not come into existence, and movie stars could not yet appear on them revealing how foolish, insipid, politically naive, psychologically tortured, vain, or stupid many of them were.

Certainly they did not, while in the midst of their careers, write memoirs about how their fathers had sexually abused them or their mothers' drinking crushed their spirits, or how they defeated their drug or alcohol problems, or screwed everyone on the set during the movie for which they narrowly missed winning an Oscar. Only their good deeds, their putatively happy family lives, their charitable works, their heroics during the war were revealed. The studios kept them tightly wrapped not in cotton, but in cashmere.

Still, actors of that era—the 1930s through the 1950s—were able to do charm in a way that has not been duplicated in our own. Julia Roberts is no replacement for Audrey Hepburn, George Clooney for Cary Grant. As immensely talented as Meryl Streep may be—she, surely, is the actor of the current age, male or female—she cannot bring off the charm of natural refinement that Deborah Kerr was able to do in movie after movie. Nor does one any longer hear, as one heard from Ronald Colman, Douglas Fairbanks Jr., Laurence Olivier, Alec Guinness, and David Niven, the charming sonorities of upper-class English accents. As for Myrna Loy, William Powell, Jean Arthur, and William Holden, movie parts featuring charm of the kind they displayed are no longer being written. Might it be that no one today is alive with a firm enough grasp of charm to write them? So strong were these models of charm provided by the movies, so compelling in performance, that in later years the novelist and philosopher Albert Camus was pleased to be thought to look and be like Humphrey Bogart and went about in a trench coat, a Bogartian cigarette dangling from his lips, while Jean-Paul Sartre fantasized being Gary Cooper—a stretch if ever there was one—his almost precise opposite physically and mentally. These compelling models of charm are no longer available, except via Turner Classic Movies.

What we were offered was pure charm unbesmirched by public scandal or personal turmoil. Not that scandalous or dreadful behavior didn't go on. How could it not? The combination of fame and vast sums of money that a successful movie career brought made egregious behavior more likely than not. Clark Gable is said to have had an illegitimate child; Myrna Loy had four marriages; Humphrey Bogart, according to Billy Wilder, was an anti-Semite even though married to a Jewish woman (Lauren Bacall, née Betty Persky) and a man with a wet palate who spat when he spoke. Most uncharming, all of this, but who knew? Who wanted to know?

What does it mean that the charm seen in the movies was not available to the actors who imitated it so charmingly on the screen? Does it disqualify charm itself as a fake, a fraud? I don't think so. One might wish that Errol Flynn were as charming a rogue off-camera as on (off-camera, he turns out to have been a bit of a creep), or that Lauren Bacall was as witty and satinly sophisticated in real as in movie life (in interviews in her later years she came across as complaining, slightly contemptuous, irritating even), but, somehow, that does not disqualify the ideals of charm, male and female, that each represented in the movies. That most of the actors who so flawlessly exhibited charm on screen were less than perfectly charming off-camera is a touch sad but not altogether shocking.

In life, charm can be a quick, a fleeting thing—represented by the perfect bit of repartee, the touch of elegant manners, the generous gesture—but in the movies charm is sustained by repetition and careful presentation. One went to the movies in search of charm—also in search of action, romance, thrills, and laughter—and more times than not found it, locking in our notions of what is charming for life.

The Hollywood definition of charm survives in the minds of most people. By this definition charm is urbane, suave, sophisticated, amusing, adult. Yet the movie stars who set this definition attained their greatest fame from the 1930s through the 1950s. Charm in the movies seemed to end sometime in the 1960s—as it tended to do in America and perhaps Western societies generally. The 1960s tended to be iconoclastic, and traditional charm was among the icons it smashed. Romantic comedy, the major vehicle for charm in the movies, all but disappeared. Tom Hanks, Steve Martin, George Clooney, Meg Ryan, Michelle Pfeiffer, Goldie Hawn played in movies, many of them written and directed by Nora Ephron, that were meant to carry on this tradition, but these movies didn't quite carry the same payload of charm that the earlier movies did. Something was missing. Might it have been the belief in charm itself?

CHAPTER II

The Standard for Charm

OF COURSE THERE WAS CHARM LONG BEFORE THE MOVIES. DIFFERENT HIS-torical ages have had different conceptions of what is charming. What charmed in the court of Louis XIV at Versailles would not have charmed at the Lyndon Johnson White House. What charms in Manhattan isn't likely to charm in Duluth, Minnesota. What charms at a cocktail party at the Brookings Institution in Washington, DC, doesn't figure to do so at a similar party at the Heritage Foundation in the same town. Different ages, different places in the same age, will have distinctly different notions of what constitutes charm.

Yet perhaps at all times a baseline has existed even to begin to qual-ify as charming. A charming person is never affected; nor is he crudely indiscreet (subtly indiscreet is a different matter); he takes into consider-ation to whom and where and under what circumstances he is displaying his charm; he does not, out of ambition or vanity, push himself forward, extolling his own talent or ability or recounting his accomplishments or triumphs. He has tact; he is only tactless on those rare occasions when tactlessness is called for. A charming person, at a minimum, has strong notions of decency and is endowed with good judgment, at least in the social realm.

In an online posting I not long ago came across, the answer to the question of what constitutes charm is set out in simple terms. "What is charm?" the posting asks. "It's that special appeal some people exude. Even those who are not particularly attractive or sexy, but have loads of charm, seem to radiate something so special that others are drawn to them. Think Tom Hanks, Oprah Winfrey and Diane Sawyer. How do they do it?"

Some among us think Tom Hanks or Oprah Winfrey and Diane Sawyer not especially charming at all. We think Tom Hanks, in his movie roles at least, likeable at best. The all but nationwide attraction of Oprah is for us one of the great mysteries of the Western world; and Diane Sawyer, dripping as she generally is with empathy, is rather heavy-going in her attempt to come across—as in a charmless age one is permitted to say—as altogether too fucking sensitive.

The online posting goes on to offer five qualities or traits that, cumulatively, constitute charm. These are 1. A sense of humor, 2. Insight and passion (an odd coupling), 3. Effortless social grace, 4. An interest in others, and 5. Curiosity about the world. The terms, as noted, are indeed simple. But are they also convincing?

Think now of Oscar Levant, who was considered one of the charming men of his day, between the 1930s and 1960s, a habitué of talk shows and television panels with a television show of his own in Los Angeles. Levant had only the first of these qualities and perhaps a dab of the second. He made himself charming by featuring his neuroses and his outrageousness. "I knew Doris Day when she was still a virgin," he said. "Schizophrenia beats dining alone," he said. "Underneath this flabby exterior," he said, "is an enormous lack of character." He also said: "I have no trouble with my enemies. It's my goddamn friends that keep me walking the floors at night." And: "Once I've made up my mind, I'm full of indecision."

Known for his quick wit and wildly imaginative put-downs, Oscar Levant was also astonishingly unpredictable—in conversation he cheated expectations, one of the marks of charm not generally noted—and could say anything at any time. He was, then, charming without passion, effortless social grace, an interest in others, and curiosity about the world. ("I have given up reading books," he said. "I find it takes my mind off myself.") If he had all these four qualities, who can say, Oscar Levant might have been a bore.

Charming people tend not only to be charming in their behavior but often to have charming stories told about them. Oscar Levant, again, qualifies here. The playwright S. N. Behrman, who knew Greta Garbo, tells of Levant's sorely wanting to meet her. Behrman told Levant that he could arrange it, but it would take time, for he had carefully to prepare the way. So each time he was with Greta Garbo, Behrman would manage to bring up the name of Oscar Levant, always remarking that he was a wonderfully amusing man, a legendary wit, legendary. Finally, the evening for the meeting arrives. Greta Garbo is to be at a dinner party at the Behrman's apartment to which Levant has also been invited. Not long after Miss Garbo arrives, Behrman brings Levant up to introduce him to her. "Greta Garbo," Behrman says, "I should like you to meet my friend Oscar Levant." Levant, so flustered by at last meeting this glamorous woman, says, "I'm sorry, I didn't quite catch your name." To which Greta Garbo, turning to Behrman, in her heavy Swedish accent, says, "Better he should remain a legend."

Charm, as I hope the case of Oscar Levant demonstrates, is too complex to be proven through a checklist of qualities. Not that everyone found Levant charming. Some people found him, with his many tics and his hypochondria, painful to watch, even on television. One had to be in on the joke—a man whose charm derives from his self-admitted, in fact highly self-advertised, neuroses—to fall under the spell of his charm.

By one criterion I can think of, Oscar Levant was distinctly not charming. A truly charming person makes you wish, however distantly, you were he or she; or if the charming person is not of your sex, that you were his or her lover or wife or husband, or in some way part of his or her life. What man of any sophistication watching the movies of Jean Arthur, or Irene Dunne, or Myrna Loy doesn't wish he had once had a love affair with her—and this no matter how much he loves his wife. Charm, as mentioned earlier, might even incur a mild form of envy. The ease of charm, the absence of strain in it, can give rise to a tinge of sadness in those who find themselves eclipsed by its light. Bringing out such a tincture of envy might even be one of the telltale signs of the charming man or woman.

Our models, which is to say our basic notions, about what constitutes charm, sometimes derive from people we are lucky enough to know, or whom we run into on our social round. More frequently they derive from literature and, in the modern era, more likely and most emphatically as I set out in my previous chapter, from the movies.

History of course provides many models of charm and so does religion. Perhaps the world's first recorded charming person was Joseph, the Biblical Joseph, the eleventh of Jacob's twelve sons. When we first encounter Joseph, his delight in his own beauty and in his confident sense of being his father's favorite fills him with overweening pride, which exhibits itself in a heedless and disagreeable braggadocio. So offensive is his vain presentation of himself that his older brothers, half out of envy and half out of simple distaste, fall on him, beat him badly, and throw him down a well, leaving him for dead. When a passing traveling merchant recovers Joseph and brings him to his brothers, they sell him into slavery to the merchant who will in turn sell him into the household of Potiphar, one of Pharaoh's chief lieutenants and a man of great power in Egypt.

At the court of Potiphar, Joseph's charm, as we should say today, kicks in. He learns to insinuate himself with the powerful. First he does so with the servant who runs Potiphar's household, eventually making himself indispensable to him and, when this servant dies, to Potiphar himself. Such is Joseph's natural charm, a charm that for women includes his good looks, that Potiphar's wife sets out to seduce him. She is unable to do so, but Joseph's enemies in Potiphar's household, supported by Potiphar's wife's vengefulness at being spurned, succeed in having him dragged off to prison.

In prison Joseph charms his jailer, and while there makes a prophesy about two of Pharaoh's leading servants, also consigned to prison, that gives him a reputation for accurate divination. Through a complicated web of incident, this power of Joseph's will bring him directly to the attention of Pharaoh, for whom he prophesies Egypt will be visited with seven fat and seven lean years. Pharaoh, whom he also charms, makes Joseph his principal administrator in planning for the seven lean years, harvesting and harboring sufficient wheat to get Egypt through them, which he does successfully. Joseph turns out to be a magnificent administrator, efficient and evenhanded, but without his charm this talent would never have emerged, nor been recognized, nor would he have become one of the heroic figures of the *Old Testament*.

Christianity does not feature charm as one of its important qualities. In the *New Testament,* charity, kindness, forgiveness reign supreme. Not that there aren't charming Christian figures among the saints. One thinks of St. Francis of Assisi, whose gentle ways charmed even the animals into trusting and loving him. Or in modern times one thinks of the Abbé Mugnier (1853–1944), the Jesuit priest admired by Marcel Proust and Paul Valery and J-K Huysmans and Jean Cocteau, and known for his sweetness of character and charming witticisms. When once asked how he, kindly and gentle man that he was, could believe in hell, the Abbé responded that he believed in hell because his church required him to believe in it, but he also believed that there was nobody in it.

Or consider Evelyn Waugh, a man who set himself up to be as comically uncharming as possible. When a woman he had offended upbraided him by saying that he was one of the rudest and most inconsiderate men she had ever met and, being so, how could he consider himself a Christian, Waugh responded: "Ah, yes, Madame, but just think what I might be like if I weren't a Christian." Waugh said many charming things, but most of these were in the nature of put-downs, nicely laced with malice, more amusing to read or hear about than to witness firsthand and not at all amusing to be the target of. Evelyn Waugh was many things, but charming wasn't among them.

During the Renaissance an attempt was made in a work called *The Book of the Courtier* by Baldassare Castiglione (1478–1529) to catalog the qualities and traits that constitute charm. A diplomatist and friend of Raphael, who painted a dazzling portrait of him, Castiglione's book was an international best-seller in its day, and was used for centuries afterward for the training of noblemen. Set out as a series of conversations between various men and women at the court of the Duke of Urbino, the most elegant court of its day among the city-states of Italy, the book asks what makes for the perfect gentleman and sets out the attributes and special talents required. The word *charm* never comes up, but is nonetheless there, the unspoken goal behind much of Castiglione's advice.

Until Castiglione's time, the perfect courtier was essentially a warrior, with bravery being the first requisite of the successful nobleman. Without degrading bravery, Castiglione wrote to suggest that a great deal more was entailed. Charm, he felt, was also needed—the kind of charm that derives from self-cultivation. Because it is self-cultivated, and not an inborn quality, the possession of charm, for Castiglione, was not restricted to the well-born. Charm of the kind Castiglione establishes and then vaunts in *The Book of the Courtier* is thus, theoretically, available to all who seek it.

Perhaps this is the place to add that charm tends to be classless, and not restricted to the rich (alas, some of the most charmless people going), or highly educated (ditto) or the otherwise well-born. In its various aspects, charm shows up across class lines—Groucho Marx was the son of a tailor, Barbara Stanwyck was raised in foster homes—ignoring sexual orientation, race, and all other social divisions. Charm turns up in unlikely places, distributed with no known bias across class or any other socially drawn lines.

To return to the perfect courtier—let us henceforth call him "the charming man"—he is, according to Castiglione, "genial and discreet," also "full of grace in all he says and does." He has good judgment in utterance, always knowing to whom he is speaking, aware of how far he can and cannot go. He outstrips others in general talent, but only by a little, lest he make them feel abashed. He never lapses into affectation, nor on the other hand does he play the jolly good fellow. He is witty, but his witticisms are without malice. In his conversation he is never predictable. He has knowledge of foreign languages, of literature and visual art, and in an amateur way, he plays musical instruments. He has a fund of amusing anecdotes, and is the source of laughter among his auditors. He is, in short, skillful at everything he does, but never pushes his skill to the point of establishing too great expertise. Castiglione underlines this point nicely with the following paragraph on chess, which one of his courtiers describes as being "certainly a pleasing and ingenious amusement," but that has one defect, which is

> . . . that it is possible to have too much knowledge of it, so that whoever would excel in the game must give a great deal of time to it, as I believe, and as much study as if he would learn some noble science or perform well anything of importance; and yet in the end, for all his pains, he only knows how to play a game.

The larger point here for Castiglione is that the charming man or woman always wants to seem casual in his attainments—to hide any signs of effort that have gone into his acquiring them and the art behind them. The notion the charming man wishes to convey is that his charm derives more from nature and inherent genius than from art. His bywords are *sprezzatura* and *disinvoltura*, the nonchalance and ease that "conceals all art and makes whatever is done or said appear to be without effort and almost without any thought about it." In his conversation, in his calm and casual performance of his skills, in all that he does, he strives (quietly, subtly) never to "produce tedium or satiety," so that he may "continually give pleasure." Never to produce tedium or satiety, continually to give pleasure—that is a definition of charm that holds up nicely in our day.

Centuries later, in *The Idea of the University* (1852), John Henry Newman describes the gentleman, who sounds a fair amount like Castiglione's courtier. Perfect courtier or true gentleman, both, in the passage below, sound like the charming man.

> *Hence it is that it is almost a definition of a gentleman to say that he is one who never inflicts pain. This description is both refined and, as far as it goes, accurate. He is mainly occupied in merely removing the obstacles which hinder the free and unembarrassed action of those about him; and he concurs with their movements rather than takes the initiative himself. His benefits may be considered as parallel to what are called comforts or conveniences in arrangements of a personal nature; like an easy chair or a good fire, which do their part in dispelling cold and fatigue, though nature provides both means of rest and animal heat without them. The true gentleman in like manner carefully avoids whatever may cause a jar or a jolt in the minds of those with whom he is cast—all clashing of opinion, or collision of feeling, all restraint, or suspicion, or gloom, or resentment; his great concern being to make everyone at his ease and at home. He has his eyes on all his company; he is tender towards the bashful, gentle towards the distant, and merciful towards the absurd; he can recollect to whom he is speaking; he guards against unseasonable allusions, or topics which may irritate; he is seldom prominent in conversation, and never wearisome. He makes light of favors while he does them, and seems to be receiving when he is conferring. He never speaks of himself except when compelled, never defends himself by a mere retort; he has no ears for slander or gossip,*

is scrupulous in imputing motives to those who interfere with him, and interprets everything for the best. He is never mean or little in his disputes, never takes unfair advantage, never mistakes personalities or sharp saying for arguments, or insinuates evil which he dare not say out. From a long-sighted prudence, he observes the maxim of the ancient sage, that we should ever conduct ourselves towards our enemy as if he were one day to be our friend. He has too much good sense to be affronted at insults, he is too well employed to remember injuries, and too indolent to bear malice. He is patient, forbearing, and resigned, on philosophical principles; he submits to pain, because it is inevitable, to bereavement, because it is irreparable, and to death, because it is his destiny.

If not always in life, one comes upon accounts of charming people in the memoirs, autobiographies, and essays of other people. Sometimes these accounts are not firsthand; all in any case have to be taken on faith. The nineteenth-century literary critic Charles Augustin Sainte-Beuve, writing about Madame de Caylus, who flourished at the Versailles court of Louis XIV, notes that she was born with natural curiosity and great wit and a perfect sense of the proprieties. "She spread about her a joy that was so gentle and so vivid, a taste for pleasure so noble and so elegant, that all characters seemed loveable and happy, so surprising is the power or rather the magic of a woman who possesses true charm."

Such claims have been made for many French women in the seventeenth and eighteenth century, especially in the period between 1750 and the Revolution of 1789, when many of the leading figures of the French Enlightenment gathered in the Parisian salons of aristocratic French women. Madame du Deffand, who counted Voltaire and Horace Walpole among her admirers and the guests in whose salon included Edmund Burke, Charles James Fox, and Edward Gibbon; Madame d'Epinay, whose salon was regularly attended by Rousseau; Julie de Lespinasse, who attracted the interest of Jean le Rond D'Alembert and David Hume— such women were connoisseurs of charm, often dazzling practitioners of wit and intellectual penetration in their own right. The magnet of their charm is what drew in the important writers and thinkers of the age to their salons. Some had intellectual charm, some emotional charm, but charm was the *sine qua non* possessed by all.

Writers of the past offer examples of charm, sometimes in their works, sometimes in their letters, not infrequently in anecdotes about them. Often they are writers whom the world has decided are minor, but whose power of conveying pleasure is nonetheless major. Sydney Smith (1771–1845) is such a writer. A clergyman, one of the founders of the *Edinburgh Review*, a man of towering common sense, Sydney Smith seems to have charmed all whom he encountered. Through his writings he charmed, among others, Queen Victoria, Charles Dickens, and Abraham Lincoln. "I sat next to Sydney Smith," Benjamin Disraeli wrote in his diary of an evening out in London, "who was delightful . . . I don't remember a more agreeable party." This seems to have been a standard reaction to this portly, unpretentious English clergyman.

After Sydney Smith's death, his wife, writing about her husband for the memory of their grandchildren, noted: "I do not believe that anyone filing only a subordinate rank in life ever past thro' it more universally beloved, more sought after for his brilliancy and wit, his honorable bearing, his masterly talents, his truth, his honesty [than your grandfather]."

Mrs. Smith's reference to "subordinate rank in life" refers to her husband's never rising very high in the clergy, which wasn't possible for a man of his strongly Whiggish views and mischievous wit. (A series of satirical compositions called *The Peter Plymley Letters*, in favor of a Catholic emancipation, were said to have kept Sydney Smith from acquiring a bishopric.) Whether he found himself, amidst the "odious smells, barbarous sounds, bad suppers" of Edinburgh, or buried in the remote fastness of a country parish, Sydney Smith found happiness. "In short," he wrote to his friend Lady Holland, "if my lot be to crawl, I will crawl contentedly; if to fly, I will fly with alacrity; but as long as I can possibly avoid it I will never be unhappy."

Not that Sydney Smith could ever be taken for one of those "cock-eyed optimists," in the Rodgers and Hammerstein sense, for he had a most precise sense of the world's imperfection. On the subject of education, for example, he believed that "the honest and orthodox method is to prepare young people for the world, as it actually exists; to tell them that they will often find vice perfectly successful, virtue exposed to a long train of afflictions; that they bear this patiently, and to look to another world for its rectification."

Sydney Smith's reputation derives as much, perhaps more, from his conversation as from his writing. Conversation is writing on sand, destined to disappear, yet so sparking was his that people seemed unable to forget it. "The fanciful and inexhaustible humorous drollery of his conversation among his intimates can never be adequately rendered," the actress Fanny Kemble said of Sydney Smith's dazzling talk. People averred that after a session with him you remembered not so much what he said but how hard you laughed. As a conversationalist, he never sought to dominate, though with him in the room others naturally tended to be a touch diffident. Walking out one day with a friend, he noted two women arguing, each from her apartment across a narrow Glasgow alley. "They can never agree," he noted, "for they are arguing from different premises." His tendency was to get on what we should today call "a roll": an anecdote leading to a pun, the pun to an aphorism, the aphorism to an amusing non sequitur, thence on to another anecdote. No one is reported ever to have had his fill of Sydney Smith's talk.

If the best comedians are thought to operate out of a fund of buried melancholy, this was also partially true of Sydney Smith. In a letter to his friend Lady Georgiana Morpeth, that begins "No one has suffered more from low spirits than I have done," he offered what he took to be his own program for combatting melancholy. This included living "as well as you dare"; taking baths with water at a low enough temperature to give a slight sensation of cold; making "no secret of low spirits to your friends, but talk of them freely—they are always the worse for dignified concealment"; not being "too severe on yourself or underrate yourself, but do yourself justice"; and, finally, taking "short views of human life—not further than dinner or tea."

Sydney Smith also felt that "pleasure is very reflective, and if you give it you will feel it." The ultimate source of his charm was his unstintingly amused response to the richness and variety and comedy inherent in life. Within his own circle of friends, no one gave more pleasure than this charming man.

Most of us have never met a Sydney Smith, or anyone in the least comparable, nor been able to attend charmed circles of the kind established by the *salonnieres* of the *ancien regime*, or been in the presence of overpowering charm. What we have all experienced, however, is the simulacrum of charm as presented in the movies. These are models, of course, as I have noted, at a second, sometimes a third remove from reality. But vivid models they were. Not long ago on television, I heard an older woman, married five times, regret that she had never really found the man for whom in her imagination she had longed. "I guess I never met anyone who treats you like Cary Grant," she said, "who talks likes James Mason, who wears clothes like Tyrone Power."

Nor is she likely to do so today, when men sit in quite good restaurants wearing baseball caps, waiters tell you their first names and that you have ordered very intelligently, children call recently met grown-ups by their first names, everyone refers to everyone else as "guys." Things as a result may be a lot more comfortable, no doubt, easygoing perhaps; but distinctly not charming, no, very far from charming.

The old standard for charm, as set by Baldassare Castiglione (never to "produce tedium or satiety . . . continually give pleasure") and John Henry Cardinal Newman ("tender towards the bashful, gentle towards the distant, and merciful towards the absurd") still exists, but begins to appear dimmer and dimmer as it recedes into the past.

CHAPTER III

What Is and Isn't Charming

"YOU KNOW WHAT CHARM IS," ALBERT CAMUS WRITES IN *THE FALL*. "A way of getting the answer yes without having asked any clear question." This subtle formulation suggests that there is always an element of con in charm. Behind such a definition lurks the notion that charm is itself inherently manipulative, carries an ulterior motive, is perhaps devious. Camus' notion of charm holds that, far from giving simple pleasure, charm is something to be on the alert against. In this interpretation, the answer to "why is this person so charming?" may come down to little more than asking, "What is he or she trying to get from me?" The charmer, as Camus had it, wants our "Yes," but yes to what? To anything from selling us a car to landing us in his or her bed, and a great deal else in between. As Carl von Clausewitz is supposed to have said, "War is diplomacy by other means," so can charm seem—and sometimes, alas, be—a con game by other means, little more.

Charm, for Camus, and for many others, was a major weapon in the arsenal of seduction, and not sexual seduction alone. The root meaning of seduction is to lead someone astray, to do something he or she either doesn't want or ought not to do. Other seductive weapons, to be sure, are available, many of them long before implanted in those of us ready to be seduced: among them appeals to greed, vanity, excessive credulity. This makes life easier for the charmer-seducer, who need know only how to turn these weaknesses to his or her own advantage.

Charm in this sense, as seduction with an ulterior motive, is obviously always to be guarded against. Easier, of course, said than done.

For seductive charmers, if they are any good, specialize in hiding their motives. One only knows one has been charmed after the trap is closed, the deal signed, one's clothes are off, the cow has been removed from the barn and you are left with only a few seeds for a beanstalk in your hand.

Others have gone even further in their criticism of charm. Toward the end of Evelyn Waugh's (immensely charming) novel *Brideshead Revisited*, the character Anthony Blanche, said to be modeled on the aesthete Harold Acton, warns the novel's narrator Charles Ryder about the evils of charm. "I took you out to dinner to warn you about charm. I warned you expressly and in great detail about the Flyte family [the occupants and owners of the grand mansion Brideshead]. Charm is the great English blight . . . It spots and kills anything it touches. It kills love; it kills art; I greatly fear, my dear Charles, it has killed you." At the same dinner Blanche tells Charles that he is an artist (a painter, readers of the novel will recall) and as such not exquisite, for true artists are not, in his view, charming. He adds: "Of course those that have charm don't really need brains." They get by, after all, on their charm. The worst that can be said against charm—and Anthony Blanche, not at all by the way, one of Evelyn Waugh's most charming characters, says it—is that it can be empty, ignorant, and destructive of more serious things.

Charm need not be either a con or be superficial. Nor ought it to be confused with the notion of cool. Cool has a linguistic history that makes evident its difference from charm, and it doesn't come near covering the richer, more complicated case of charm. The origin of the word *cool* in its approbative sense is attributed to Lester Young, the tenor saxophonist; its context was the dignified performance of African-American jazz musicians in the face of crude racialist laws. The use of cool, too, has been subject to wrenching changes. Cool once attached to the easy elegance of Duke Ellington or Lena Horne. In the 1960s and '70s, though, cool often meant being against authority, otherwise known as "the system"; or having the blind courage to experiment with LSD. Cool meant Marlon Brando on a motorcycle or James Dean mumbling inchoately—cool, yes, perhaps, but distinctly not charming. Cool always meant being in control, if not of anything in the external world, then certainly of oneself. The cool person, as they used to say, "had it all together," with the meaning of the antecedentless "it" always more than a touch less than clear.

Charm is social; cool tends to be, if not antisocial then above any interest in winning approval. Cool in its more recent sense is above all detached. In the 1950s, James Dean was cool; in the 1960s Steve McQueen was cool; Patti Smith was cool in the 1970s, and for many still is today; Kurt Cobain and Madonna were cool in the '80s and '90s. Frank Sinatra and Dean Martin were thought cool through more than a single decade, as was Paul Newman. All of these people had about them the implied notion that they were not to be trifled with or otherwise put upon; some even suggested an element of danger if one were to attempt to get too close to them. The jazz trumpeter Miles Davis is perhaps the best example of this last kind of cool, cool with an edge to it of potential cruelty, possibly danger. Very far, all this, from charming.

Elegance is another quality sometimes confused with charm. Charming people are often elegant, though today standards in elegance are themselves highly uncertain. Elegance can sometimes be as off-putting as it can be in-gathering. Of a snobbish writer of the 1920s and '30s named Lucius Beebe a journalist once noted that he "was menacingly well dressed." Of Beebe's formal manners, a woman friend remarked, when he went into the hospital for surgery, "I do hope the surgeon has the common decency to open Lucius at room temperature," a story that is more charming than the man who was its subject. Elegant manners, invented to lubricate sociability, can also be used to chill it. Yet elegance, when made to seem natural, can, and often does, aid or supplement charm. Too many not especially elegant people, and some who have been deliberately inelegant—see my chapter on Vulgar Charmers—have been charming for elegance to be one of charm's hallmarks.

Amusing is another word that is often tossed up in searching for a definition of charm. Most people who are charming are also often amusing but not all amusing people are charming. In our day the comedians Sarah Silverman and Louis CK can be amusing but are not especially charming; in fact they are sometimes, quite purposefully, vile. Monkeys can be amusing, but one would scarcely think to call them charming. Charm has a larger circumference than amusement; and rightly so, for much more goes on within the circle of charm.

Charm is sometimes thought sexy, which it can be, and it can of course lead on to sex, which it sometimes does. But sexy, in itself, isn't especially charming. Glands and hormones and private parts do not register charm. Has anyone ever written charming pornography? Philip Roth attempted comic pornography, and with some success. Henry Miller also intermittently succeeded in this line. I recall from the halcyon days of literary censorship when as a college kid I read in one of Miller's banned novels, in their Olympia Press plain green covers, a scene in which Miller describes making love to a woman standing up in a hallway, in the midst of which he wrote, as I remember, something like, "Her purse fell to the floor. A coin dropped out. I made a mental note to pick it up later." Such comic touches, though, were washed away by scores of pages given over to Miller's boringly earnest pornography.

One can begin to build up a negative definition of charm by specifying various human qualities that get in the way of, if they not positively prevent, charm. People who are argumentative are not charming. People who too obviously show their vanity cannot be charming. Neither can those who name-drop egregiously. Legion are the numbers of people who overestimate their charm, and doing so is perhaps among the most common of all social errors.

True charm does have an element of irresistibility. People are drawn to it. In *Sunset and Twilight*, his final diary volume, Bernard Berenson speaks of a cousin who he thinks of "as a partner in the wide-flung firm of 'Charm Incorporated.'" This cousin is also a favorite "in ultra-smart society," who knows wealthy Greeks (Onassis, Niarchos, and so on) and central figures in the Eisenhower administration. He is offered jobs, is everywhere welcome. Berenson mentions another of his acquaintances who is a member of Charm Incorporated, Georges Salles, a Jew who is the grandson of Gustave Eiffel, the Alsatian who designed and constructed the Eiffel Tower, and a man welcomed everywhere he goes, and among those "who no doubt have capacities, and even merits, but nothing like (equal to) the rewards they garner." Salles held several high-level curatorial jobs in France and was, Berenson reports, "a sugarplum for hungry but beau-

tiful women his life long, and still so, I dare say. What a successful career!"
And all built on charm.

Men and women have always existed who get by on their charm.
Sometimes they have talent and skill and character to go with it, sometimes not. The trick the charming person can sometimes turn is to make
himself seeming winning, whether he truly is or not. How does he or she
do it? Various, as I hope to show, are the ways.

The charming person is not opinionated, at least not openly so. In
conversation he is often more interested, or at least shows himself more
interested, in hearing your opinions than in expressing his own. He never
pushes nor advertises himself, certainly not in any aggressive or obvious
way. He often has the gift of intimacy, of making you feel that the two
of you are close, tight, members under the skin of that select little club
E. M. Forster called "the aristocracy of the sensitive, the considerate, and
the plucky."

If the charming person is neither argumentative nor opinionated, this
means that he is probably not very political. Like everyone else, he may
have his political views, but they are not central to his personality—not, at
least, if he wishes to remain charming. Certainly he does not consider his
political views the source of his virtue. For him virtue lies elsewhere: in
kindness, generosity, graciousness, considerateness. Instead of opinions, he
not so much professes as exhibits, gently, always understatedly, a point of
view, which provides a complex, interesting outlook on the world.

William Bolitho (1890–1930), a now forgotten essayist, is said to have
been a spellbinding conversationalist. Walter Lippmann remembered him as
"seizing command of the discussion and transporting it quickly to regions
where even the most debilitating bore was too uncertain of himself to do
anything but listen." Lippmann explains why so conversationally dominant
a man wasn't himself a bore: "Because he was so instantly aware of all who
were present, seeing them not as silhouettes but in the round and often clair-
voyantly, he made them all share the excitement which he has in exploring
his own thoughts. They would go home feeling not only that they had
heard a brilliant performance, but that they had been rather uncommonly
brilliant themselves." Yet one wonders if Bolitho wasn't too brilliant—one
wonders if dazzling, as he seems to have been, is quite the same as charming.

How many evenings with the enchanting Mr. Biltho could one take? The charming person, true enough, often does make everyone around him feel, depending on the nature of his charm, more brilliant, amusing, lively, ultimately charming himself. And yet those charmers who dominate any room they inhabit are in danger of themselves becoming tiring and ultimately tiresome. One can, after all, become overcharmed.

The charming person may be entertaining, but never that full-time thing, an entertainer, with the latter's need for constant attention and approval. Which is perhaps why Oscar Wilde, who said so many amusing things, always playing to the gallery—"Bernard," Wilde told Bernard Berenson, "you forget that in every way I want to imitate my Maker, and like him I want nothing but praise"—was probably not finally charming. With his endless epigrams, ripostes, paradoxes, the old boy called attention to himself no matter where he was. ("I have nothing to declare but my genius," he is said to have told the customs officials upon his arrival in 1892 for a lecture tour of the United States.) Doubtless he was entertaining; but doubtless, too, he must have used up all the oxygen in the room, every room, he entered where there was company to impress.

Suavity, urbanity, sophistication can be constituent parts of charm, yes; pushing oneself forward as the ego urges, clearly not. "Look at me" can never be the banner under which the charmer travels. ("What would be the use of culture," Goethe remarks, "if we did not try to control our natural tendencies.") The charming person wishes to please without any suggestion of showing off. He does so without ever falling into unctuousness, flattery, ingratiation. While charm isn't about mere agreeableness, the charming person, though he may when required beg to differ, is never truly disagreeable.

Charm often carries an amiable, an admirable detachment. The charming person seems to have an amused—and amusing—*coin de vantage*, or angle on things. A glass of wine in his hand, a touch aloof, but never off-puttingly so, he steps in to make a casual but telling observation, offers a witty remark, formulates rather better than anyone else what is really on everyone else's mind. If a short definition of charm is wanted, charm is that person, man or woman, whom you never want to leave the room.

Let's recollect our fundamental, our *Oxford English Dictionary*, definition of charm, which is "providing delight . . . arousing approval." Stare at this definition long enough and one begins to see not merely a definition but implicit in it an interpretation of charm. Does the charming person provide delight, the definition ever so faintly suggests, chiefly to arouse approval? And this approval, once aroused and won, to what uses might it be put? Those suspicious of charm would say none worth admiring.

I suspect that the truly charming person does not think of approval as his primary goal. He charms because he cannot help himself. He charms because it gives him pleasure to please. He can no more turn off the charm than the boorish man can turn it on. Charm, like goodness, becomes ingrained. When it works, there is no defense against it. Nor, when it is motiveless, need there be. When one is lucky enough to encounter charm, in a friend, a new acquaintance, a movie, a writer, a singer, a song, the best response is merely to take it in, to enjoy it. Charming—the word itself has a lovely soothing ring; and the quality itself, when it turns up to the right power, can be, more than soothing, enchanting.

CHAPTER IV

Who Isn't Charming?

I HAVE ASKED A NUMBER OF FRIENDS AND ACQUAINTANCES TO NAME FIVE persons in public life in the contemporary world whom they think charming. No one has been able to do it. Names are brought up—Tom Hanks, Meryl Streep, Vince Scully, Steve Martin, Bill Murray—but none gets anything like a consensus of agreement. Fifty years ago, names would have issued easily from anyone asked the same question: Yogi Berra, Duke Ellington, Jackie Gleason, Walter Pidgeon, Barbara Stanwyck, Louis Armstrong, Jack Benny, Dorothy Parker, and on and on. What has happened to bring about this obvious shortage of charming people?

A number of possibilities here. The first is that public figures in our day are overexposed, when notably charming figures of other times weren't exposed at all. We know too much about them—often too much of the tumult and sadness stirring beneath the burnished veneer of their outward charm. In an earlier day, before the advent of the talk show and the celebrity interview article, the private lives of public figures were allowed to remain just that, private. A movie star might be interviewed on the radio, but the subject was usually his or her current or next movie. A scandalous item might get into the gossip columns, but usually it didn't too greatly dim the brightness the studio had sedulously backlit for the star. The magazine celebrity profile, usually written for fan magazines, was controlled by the celebrity or by his or her studio or agent.

A different order of decorum was in place then than now. As personal example of the extent to which things have changed, in 1976 I wrote an article in *Chicago* magazine mocking a then locally famous gossip columnist named Irv Kupcinet. In a faux naïve manner, I inquired how a man of so little talent was able to rise so high in his line of work. In writing the article it would not have occurred to me to bring Kupcinet's family, and hence private life, to the fore. His career was fair game, but the game stopped at his private life. Thirty or so years later a journalist in the same magazine writing about the same man speculated that his wife may have been ultimately responsible for the suicide of their daughter by pushing her too hard to advance her sputtering career as an actress.

Today it is open season on movie stars, politicians, entertainers, athletes, musicians, writers. The word *icon*, generally and sloppily denoting an extremely well-known public figure, seems to have been invented in part to remind us of the root meaning of the word *iconoclast*, a smasher of icons. In such a journalistic atmosphere, the one in which we have for a long while now been living, it isn't easy for a public figure to retain his or her dignity, let alone the high gloss of his or her (often studio or public-relations created) charm.

Quite possibly many of the figures we took fifty or more years ago to be charming, under the closer inspection of our day would have shown themselves to be far from it. Clark Gable, in his day a model of masculine savoir faire, we now learn was a masher, a heavy boozer, the father of an illegitimate child with Loretta Young (whom he is said to have date raped), and a man who wore false teeth and had questionable breath. Humphrey Bogart, everyone's ideal notion of urban suavity and hence big-city charm, turns out to have been a difficult character in every way: an unpleasant wise guy with a wet palette who wore a hairpiece. The director Billy Wilder in an interview with Cameron Crowe recounts working with Bogart on *Sabrina*. In the interview he asserts that Bogart was touchy and envious and spat when he spoke. "He was a shit," Wilder says, though later he allows that Bogart was brave in the face of his death by cancer. Read that and the famous Bogart charm leaks away.

My friend Hilton Kramer told me that, when he was the art critic for the *New York Times,* he was at the Los Angeles County Art Museum to write up a current show. Before he set out on his tour of the works he was to write about, the director of the museum informed him that Edward G. Robinson, himself a notable collector of old masters, was in the museum, and would like nothing better than to accompany Hilton as he walked through the building. Hilton said that he greatly admired the movies of Edward G. Robinson, that Robinson was easily his favorite Hollywood actor, and few things would give him more pleasure than to have the great movie star join him on his tour. "Within ten minutes," Hilton said, "I had only one question: How can I get rid of this guy, who felt the need to rehearse every platitude about visual art known to man." More of a sad than a comic story, this, I think.

One cannot go poking around in the private lives of public figures and expect many to survive the investigation altogether intact. Cary Grant would be on everyone's short list of great charmers. And so he was—as Cary Grant the Hollywood star. Not long ago the actor Frank Langella published a memoir, *Dropped Names: Famous Men and Women,* in which he reports Tony Curtis remarking of Grant—whose screen presence Curtis originally hugely admired—that he "was a fucking bore, who sucked the air out of any room he was in." Other people soon chimed in. Mel Brooks, on television, told the story of how thrilling it was when he first arrived in Hollywood to find himself in a studio office next to Cary Grant's. The thrill increased when Grant invited him to lunch. The lunch didn't go off very well, but Brooks blamed himself. After a second lunch, he realized that the fault wasn't his. When Grant called a third time for lunch, Brooks instructed his secretary to tell the great star that he wasn't in.

The other degrading Cary Grant story has to do with his at one point sharing a house with Randolph Scott. Long before there had been rumors that Scott was gay—for what it's worth, he probably wasn't—and so suddenly the rumors about homosexuality extended to Cary Grant. They were only squelched when another person came forth to remark that homosexuality had nothing to do with the two men living together. They lived together to save money; both Scott and Grant were said to be among the cheapest men in Hollywood. Cheap, whatever else it is, isn't charming.

None of these stories would have been told to begin with if the breakdown of decorum didn't, as it now obviously does, extend into the past. Of Anne Bancroft, Mel Brooks' deceased wife, Langella tells stories about her astonishing narcissism, once being enraptured by the image of a woman seen in a department-store mirror who turned out to be herself.

In our time, one sad miscue, or serious mistake, can on the instant of its revelation, divast forever a person of his reputation for charm or even virtue. The magazine *Vanity Fair* ran an article about Arthur Miller, who always carried himself as a pillar of high integrity and keen sensitivity, and a great lover of humanity, in which it was revealed that, with his second wife, the Swedish photographer Inge Morath, he had a son with Down syndrome who, soon after his birth, he clapped into an institution and never saw again. Poof! The pillar of integrity turns into a pillar of salt. Not even the dead, including the most sacred idols among the dead, are safe from diminishment in an indecorous age.

Nor does the therapeutic spirit behind investigations into the lives of public figures conduce to the retention of charm. Sadder still, many celebrities may be said almost to specialize in revealing their own hang-ups, weaknesses, mental and physical malfunctions, abuses suffered in childhood. The journalist Tina Brown, formerly editor of *The Tatler, Vanity Fair,* and the *New Yorker,* makes this same point: "Celebrity culture has been out of control for a long time, and the more media there is, the more short-lived their staying power. When *Vanity Fair* began, it was enough to have a movie star on the cover, but Oprah made some psychic scar *de rigueur* for exposure to get any traction. Now you can't get on a talk show unless you can brag about being a victim of pedophilia or anorexia. It's such a bore, all the whining."

Politicians may seem charming, but ultimately they cannot be so, if only because, by the nature of their profession, they are divisive. The people who don't agree with their views are unlikely to find them charming—quite the reverse. The divisiveness of politicians drains them of their charm. Many people feel Barack Obama is charming, but quite as many think any charm he might possess is negated by his political ideas. Whether or not he is charming depends on the filter of political beliefs and prejudices one happens to be wearing. The same was true earlier of Franklin Delano Roosevelt, though in a charm election he would probably have had a larger plurality than Barack Obama—less than half the nation loathed him. Winston Churchill may have been the last charming politician, along with having been an authentically great man; his charm of course derived from his wit. ("Politics," he said, "is the ability to foretell what is going to happen tomorrow, next week, next month and next year. And to have the ability afterwards to explain why it didn't happen.") Conservatives found Ronald Reagan utterly charming; liberals thought him a dolt with a bad hair-dye job.

Many people found and continue to find Bill Clinton charming, despite all the scandal that has attended his career. Daniel Patrick Moynihan, a politician whom many (I among them) found charming, had a low view of the Clintons; he thought them interested finally only in getting themselves elected and ultimately more concerned about looking good than doing good. Yet, upon Moynihan's retirement, he was called upon to endorse Hillary Clinton as the candidate for his seat in the US Senate, which had to be an unappetizing chore. As a good party man, Moynihan had no choice, so he did it. While doing so, Moynihan was never less charming.

As for Bill Clinton's Monica Lewinsky scandal, some may have found it amusing, a fraternity-boy-like prank, even if taken place in the Oval Office of the President of the United States, a setting, one might have thought, of the greatest seriousness. When Clinton did his best to elude the charges against him, nobody believed him, but nobody could blame him for attempting to do so. Despite what the television reporter Cokie Roberts called the incident's "yuk factor," one need not necessarily despise Bill Clinton for this egregious lapse. I didn't—that is, until I learned that, as the evidence began to pile up against him, Clinton suggested to his White House confidants that they spread the story that the twenty-three-year-old Monica was "stalking" him. With this the screw-off fraternity boy instantly disappeared and the creep came to the fore. Not charming, no, not in the least.

In any list of charming politicians, most people would put forth the name of John F. Kennedy. Since his death, too much has become known about Kennedy, and what is known divests him of much of the charm he might once have been thought to possess. He was a philanderer of a very high power—so high as to rank as a sexual predator—while selling himself as a family man and loving father. Story after story of his activity in this line has come out since his death. The most recent, written by a former White House intern named Mimi Alford, is perhaps the most cringe-making of all. She recounts, with very little apparent malice in the telling, of Kennedy's all but raping her in the White House when she was nine-teen. He subsequently took her along on some of his political travels, a portable concubine, a sexual treadmill of sorts, leaving her awaiting him in hotel rooms while he expatiated on virtue in the public arena.

Some people might find this forgivable—emperors and kings have done no less—but Mimi Alford tells of "Mr. President," as she always called him, also requesting that she provide relief for one of his aids in the form of fellatio, which she agreed to do, and "relaxation" for his brother Teddy, which she chose not to do. "Ask what you can do for your country," the JFK inaugural speech needs to be rewritten after Ms. Alford's memoir, "while I'll be upstairs in the White House bonking a teenager." Not charming.

Celebrities and especially movie stars who might otherwise be charming put a serious dent in their charm once they declare their pol-itics. George Clooney, who many people think charming, and who is an actor in the male line of Cary Grant and Gig Young, lost much of his cachet because of too regularly making known his strong liberal views; at any rate he figures to have lost it in the view of those who oppose such views. The same might be said on the other side for Clint Eastwood's declarations of his conservatism. Jane Fonda lost much ground through her political protests during the Vietnam War, becoming Hanoi Jane, the Vietnam War's version of Tokyo Rose. Jane Fonda has always been an excellent actress, but her politics lost her, too, a good part of her audi-ence. Movie stars always had politics, but the old studio system cautioned them against announcing their politics too blatantly, if at all. In so highly politicized a country as America has become, once one does so, one loses roughly half one's potential audience. Or as the basketball player Michael Jordan, who kept his politics to himself, once put it, "Even Republicans buy gym shoes."

If I were to have asked people not to name five charming people in public life but five who overrate their charm, most would hesitate to stop at a mere five. Start with Keith Olbermann and Rush Limbaugh, on opposite sides of the political fence, but together in thinking themselves charming when they are the reverse. Let us add Regis Philbin, so patheti-cally mistaken in his assumption that he has a winning personality. Toss in

Bill Moyers, so certain of his virtue, and Bill Maher, whose idea of wit is to call someone whose politics he contemns an "asshole." Donald Trump's is a name that scarcely required saying, and was italicized during his run for the presidency and has not in the least diminished since he has attained that high office. The two retired tennis champions Jimmy Connors and John McEnroe easily make the list. Barbra Streisand is certainly on it, as are those former professional television hosts Phil Donahue and Larry King. Whoopi Goldberg and Barbara Walters are decidedly uncharming; much of the cast of the morning television show called *The View* also qualify nicely. The list could be greatly extended.

From 1950 through 1967 a television program called *What's My Line?* ran on Sunday nights in America. For those too young to remember the program, the idea behind it was for a panel of supposedly sophisticated Manhattanites to guess the strange jobs of guests and, after being blind-folded, to guess the name of a mystery guest, who was him- or herself a celebrity of one sort or another. The women wore what were then called cocktail dresses, the men were in black tie. Among the sometimes-alternating regular four panelists were the actresses Arlene Francis and Kitty Carlisle, the newspaper columnist Dorothy Kilgallen, the actors Martin Gable and Hans Conried, the comedian Steve Allen, the publisher Bennett Cerf, and George S. Kaufman, a deeply neurotic playwright and theater critic who claimed to have left psychotherapy because his therapist asked too many God-damned personal questions. The host of the show was a former newspaper executive named John Daly, whose only obvious talent or qualification for the job was a distinctly upper-class accent.

The presupposition of *What's My Line?* was its charm. We, its viewers, were, in effect, being allowed the privilege of witnessing a parlor game played by charming New Yorkers. Charmed with one another they may have been, but their collective unreality; their assumption that everyone was, like them, vastly wealthy, moderately famous, and happily urbane; their certainty of their cleverness; their clammy clubbiness, was appalling. They made one wish for a brief revolution, just long enough to see their heads roll. The show stayed on television for seventeen years. Might it have done so because it gave its viewers a fine release at the close of the week, a way to discharge distaste and even hatred, by pouring it onto these unattractive people who, mistake of mistakes, were so utterly and mistakenly confident of their charm?

Earlier, in setting out names of people who overestimate their charm, I thought about adding that of David Letterman. My guess is that the world was divided into three when it comes to David Letterman: those who adored him, those who deplored him, and those who could not care less about him. I tend to fall into the third category, but I cannot help comparing him to his predecessor, Johnny Carson, who was charming enough to last fully thirty years as the so-called host of *The Tonight Show*.

Part of Carson's charm was in his talent at selflessness and at self-abasement. Watching him on television over the years, one felt a certain generosity of spirit in him in his being pleased when other comedians succeeded on his show, a pleasure that one gathers is far from standard behavior in show business. Carson never seemed to push himself forward, and only talked about himself in a joking, self-degrading way. He joked about his drinking during his bachelor days, or he mocked his own infelicity at marriage, having been a many-times divorced man. If he had political views, which one assumes he did, he kept them to himself.

Since Johnny Carson's death, it has been revealed, through an HBO special about him, that he had a mother, whom, however great his success, he could never please, which couldn't have been easy on him. His failed marriages, about which he joked on television, in life turned out to be, predictably, sad. But a charming man or woman would never bring such things up in company, let alone on national television, whereas a person who overestimates his charm—and also his importance—leads with them. Whatever the problems of his personal life, Johnny Carson was too charming ever to do that.

If there is anything like a single indisputable rule about charm, it is this: If you think you are charming, there is an excellent chance that you probably aren't. Most of the men and women I have mentioned in this chapter are cases in point.

CHAPTER V

Am I Charming?

FULL IN THE FACE OF MY ONE RULE ABOUT CHARM, THAT IF ONE THINKS ONE is charming one probably isn't, I wish now to say I do believe I am charming: mildly charming, and, alas, resistibly, highly resistibly, so, but still somewhat charming, I do believe, nonetheless. Mine is at best a secondary charm. (Charm, unlike pregnancy and the quality of uniqueness, admits of qualification and gradations.) I have never charmed exotic women into my bed or charmed my way into theirs. So far as I know I have never gained a job or vast sums of money or advancement of any serious kind through such charm as I may possess. The best that my charm may have brought me is a few new friends—people who, after a brief while in my company, may have noted to themselves that I seem a person of possible interest, someone mildly amusing or clever, with no obvious side to him, and is, who knows, perhaps worth knowing a little better.

I cannot recall ever having been called charming. The only evidence I have of my charm are the smiles and the laughter of family and friends and acquaintances, when I have been able to evoke them. The closest I have come in recent years to have an open avowal of my charm was made by a publisher who invited me to a very expensive dinner at a now-defunct Chicago restaurant called Charlie Trotter's. The morning after our dinner, he sent me an e-mail saying that he was miffed by the fact that our conversation was so enjoyable that he couldn't remember any of the wonderful food he had eaten the night before. A charming compliment, this, and one that suggests, now that I think about it, the publisher may well be more charming than I.

Some people are content to be charmed; others among us feel we must impose our charm, such as it is. I write "us," for I have most of my life been among those who feel it incumbent upon themselves to assert what they believe is their charm, however minor it might be, in however circumspect a manner. Why do I feel it incumbent at all? I was not a boy that girls found especially appealing. I was a respectable but less than terrific athlete. As a student, I may be said not to have existed, finishing just above the lower quarter of my high-school class. As a field of successful endeavor that left charm, or what, in my high-school days, passed for charm.

I may have picked up the notion that I was under an obligation to charm from my father, who was a salesman. "You have to sell yourself," my father used to say, and this must have been what he did in his successful career selling things he didn't know all that much about: at first linens and handkerchiefs, later costume jewelry, novelties, athletic trophies.

I doubtless picked up from my father the notion that one should make the effort to sell oneself. This entailed demonstrating, never too aggressively, that one was one of the boys, without malice or meanness, in short, in the high accolade of my youth, a good guy. "No one expects you to be an angel," my father instructed me, "but that doesn't give you a warrant to be an s.o.b." In a further anti-s.o.b. instruction, he said: "Never be an s.o.b., for you can never tell when you might need the help of someone lower down whom you passed on the way up." My father wasn't as calculating as I seem to be making him out to be here—he was a genuinely generous and good-hearted man—but I subconsciously took up his credo, that of being a bit of a salesman of oneself, one whose only product was charm.

Charm in the days of my adolescence took the form of being witty, good at repartee, having the ability to tell a story well. I think I passed with respectable grades at all these exercises. Perhaps the most charming thing I did as a boy, though, was listen to others. I was a sedulous listener, and genuine listening can of course contribute a good deal to the notion that one is charming. ("'Tell me,'" Max Beerbohm declared, "are the two most beautiful words in the English language.") I specialized in those days in insinuating myself with people, or at least those among them I thought worth exerting my charms upon. I wanted to be liked, I knew how to go about it, and I usually succeeded. I was, yes, a good guy, a damn good guy.

Apart from adding a few layers of sophistication and a touch or two of learning into the mix, I am not sure that such charm as I possess today is in any way different than it was in my high-school days. Such arrows as I carry in my charm quiver include what I hope are a number of interesting anecdotes, an ample fund of jokes, a certain ability to manipulate language for comic effect, occasional flashes of wit, and an amused outlook on life.

I am not the life of the party; never have been, nor yearned to be. I haven't ever had the least wish to dominate socially. At its most ambitious my charm goal has been to be one of the people who made the party a bit more pleasant by saying a few amusing things. "I met a nice man named Joe Epstein at Posey Fisher's last night," I imagine someone saying, "who did an uncanny imitation of Jackie Mason, recounted a touching story about T. S. Eliot, and told a good joke about a Soviet painter asked to do a portrait of Lenin in Warsaw."

The older one gets the greater one's chance for exercising such charm as one possesses. Men of a certain age, of whom I have for a good while been one, are no longer on the front lines in the sex wars, and can therefore say things to young women that they never could when themselves young, lest they be taken for mashers. I find myself doing it with young female bank tellers, supermarket check-out women, waitresses, and others. "That new short haircut looks marvelous on you," I might say. Or: "Very exotic that nail polish you're wearing." Or: "Those company clothes the bank makes you wear—on you they look good." Or, taking things a step further: "Ah, if I were only forty years younger, I should pursue you with all the savage cunning now at my command. Maybe I better make that fifty years younger." I say these things not merely to be nice, or to be selling, but invariably because I mean them.

Such charm as I possess is not regularly exercised on a wide social circle. I lunch with friends, and sometimes meet others for afternoon coffee. I go to few dinner parties. Cocktail parties are my notion of punishment. I am not in the least shy; am undaunted by the rich, the famous, or the powerful; and in the company of strangers do not mind establishing my bona fides as a man of the world. One of the pleasures of encountering strangers is of course that they haven't heard my stories and jokes before.

On this score, my wife of more than forty years, who has heard all of both doubtless too many times, easily qualifies as long-suffering.

In any social setting in which I find myself, I suppose I tend to do my share of the talking. Sometimes I walk away worried that I have done more than my share, have slipped over from being a contributor to the conversation to having orchestrated and conducted it. Being easily bored, I greatly fear boring others. I can easily bear to have my politics despised, my opinions refuted, my taste mocked, but being thought a bore would sting terribly.

We all know too many people who overestimate their charm. They remind one of the man who, when his wife asked upon his return from a party how things went, answered: "If it weren't for me, I'd have been bored to death." They are certain of the fascination they feel they are exerting, of how compelling they are, of how absolutely indispensable to the festivities at hand, when in fact one feels that one has heard everything they have to say or would prefer never to have heard it in the first place. To be told I am one of those people would be a serious, a withering, perhaps the greatest insult.

Anyone who has been in the company of heavy-breathing professional charmers knows that it is possible to be too charming. These are the (mostly) men who have an anecdote for every subject that arises, a joke that covers every case, lumpish bits of gossip, heavy name-dropping to spice the conversational pudding when they (mis)judge that it's needed. They are altogether too well equipped in the charm arsenal.

I wonder if my own charm, such as it is, doesn't come across better on the page than in person. In person, one can overdo charm so easily by going on too long, by getting the punch line of a story slightly askew, by misconstruing the interest of the people to whom one is talking. But writing, owing to the blessed act of revision, permits nearly endless dress rehearsal, which allows at least the possibility of getting it right, the words, the timing, the length of one's discourse. The spontaneity, which is often a substantial part of charm, may be missing, but in exchange one has the hope of achieving polish and getting nearer perfection.

Charmers can of course be manipulative, with motives and agendas of their own. Having searched my own conscience on this point, I find that my only motive as a would-be charmer is the simple—I leave it to you to judge if it is also pathetic—desire to be liked. As a writer, I've made my share of enemies, some of whom I'm proud to have as enemies, but I still prefer to think that when I wish I can make people I like like me.

"Gad," as the charming Charles Lamb wrote, "how we like to be liked."

PART TWO

Chapter VI

Charmed Lives

SOME PEOPLE APPEAR TO HAVE CHARMED LIVES. THEY ARE BORN TO WEALTH, are dazzlingly good-looking, highly intelligent, with a natural joy in life. Everything seems to be going for them, everything appears to come easily to them; nothing lies out of their reach; all their desires are readily satisfied. The number of such people may be minuscule, but when one comes upon any of them, one cannot help but yearn, at least a little, to be in their place. Envy admixes with admiration in our reaction to them.

Movie stars once seemed to live such charmed lives, with their beauty and vast salaries and their mansions and Malibu beach settings. But now, when exposé journalism and sad confession work against them, less and less so. Today a small number of athletes seem, at least from the middle distance, to lead charmed lives. Roger Federer, Derek Jeter, Michael Jordan, Joe Montana, such men seem the gifted of the gods: hugely rewarded in fame and fortune for doing exceedingly well what they love to do anyway and in front of vast admiring crowds.

Some charmed lives have sometimes had much too early endings. One thinks first of all of Mozart, a genius from the very beginning but dead at thirty-five. Or the movie producer Irving Thalberg, the only man, in F. Scott Fitzgerald's phrase, to have grasped "the whole equation" of making successful movies, who died at thirty-seven. (Fitzgerald himself died at forty-four.) Or George Gershwin, one of America's few authenic musical geniuses, who pegged out at thirty-eight. All lived full-out, under the radiant sun of their very different talents. Owing to these various talents, all had, or at least appeared to have, charmed if abbreviated lives. But,

49

then, for the ancient Greeks, in their myths and also among their living heroes, the most splendid creatures die young. See Adonis, Achilles, Alcibiades, Greek literature *passim*.

In *Charmed, A Family Romance*, his book about his father and his father's brothers, Michael Korda begins by describing the most successful of these brothers, his Uncle Alex, the Hungarian-born movie producer, by describing his traveling arrangements.

> *When my Uncle Alex traveled, he was driven straight to the steps of the airplane in his black Rolls-Royce Silver Shadow after all the other passengers had boarded. If he was late the airplane was held until he arrived; ships and trains waited for him, customs and passport formalities were arranged to suit his convenience, officials rushed to make his arrivals and departures effortless and pleasant, swiftly chalking a customs mark on his white calfskin Revelation luggage and on the brass-bound morocco traveling humidor with a dovetailed sliding lid and his initials "A.K." stamped in the fragrant leather.*

Whether this is truly charming, or merely evidence of a privileged life, is less than clear, but for Michael Korda, a man always much impressed by power and status, it is irrefutable evidence of a charmed life.

People with charmed lives tend to travel in charmed circles. Membership in the circle in itself usually confers the aura of charm. The Algonquin Circle, that gathering of writers, editors, and critics who kept a regular table at the Algonquin Hotel in Manhattan, is generally thought to have been charming. And so it was, but only if viewed from the middle distance. Much of its charm derived from the witty remarks fired off at these lunches, many of the better ones by Dorothy Parker. (Example: "Age before beauty," said Claire Booth Luce, opening a door for Miss Parker. Passing through Miss Parker retorted, "Pearls before swine.") Dorothy Parker said many amusing things, but her life, alas, was far from amusing, and even further from charming. She had a penchant for linking up with worthless men. ("I require three things in a man," she said. "He must be handsome, ruthless, and stupid.") She several times attempted suicide, she lived with small dogs in hotel rooms that she soon made squalid. She died in one of these, and, though small, had to be stood up vertically on a stretcher in the narrow elevator of one of those hotels thence to be transported to a funeral home. Not, no, distinctly not, charming. George S. Kaufman more than matched Dorothy Parker for neurotic behavior. A steady philanderer, impotent only with his wife, he told Irving Berlin he would much prefer if he retitled his song "Always" as "Thursdays." Harold Ross of the *New Yorker*, though a great editor, was a philistine. And so on. To find the Algonquin Circle charming, my guess is, it is better to read about it than to have witnessed it or to know too much about the personal lives of its members.

Other times what seem like charmed lives only mask what are sad, even tragic lives. Among Americans, no couple seemed to fit the formula of charmed lives more snugly than Gerald (1888–1964) and Sara Murphy (1883–1975). Gerald's father, Patrick, was a partner in Mark Cross, the elegant leather goods manufacturer and retailer. Sara's father was Frank Wiborg, of Cincinnati, an immensely successful manufacturer of ink and varnish. The Wiborgs lived part of the year at the Gotham Hotel in New York and part in East Hampton on their estate on Long Island, where the Murphys also kept a summer place.

This was the period of the WASP ascendancy in America, and while neither the Murphys nor the Wiborgs were, strictly speaking, WASPs, they, like the Kennedys in later years, those other non-WASPs who took the WASP model for their own, lived in the highest WASP style. Sara and her two sisters went through the torture of debutante coming out. Gerald, never a good student, struggled to get into Yale. The two families were in the same social circle on East Hampton.

Sara Wiborg was five years older than Gerald Murphy, and during their early acquaintance looked upon him as a younger brother. He seems to have adored her from the very first. Attractive, bright, adventurous, Sara Wiborg was not, in the marital line, a closer; men were attracted to her but none offered marriage. She was thirty-two, he twenty-seven, when she and Gerald married. Neither of their families approved of the marriage. In the best arriviste tradition, each family thought its child could have done better. Sara's photograph announcing their engagement was nonetheless on the cover of *Town and Country*.

Gerald Murphy was earning $3,000 a year at Mark Cross in 1917 when he married Sara Wiborg, which was the equivalent of $50,000 in our day. Her father, Frank Wiborg, was certain that his extravagant daughter could not live on so paltry a sum, so he gave her an annual allowance of $15,000, or five times her husband's salary and the equivalent of $250,000 today. They rented a house in Greenwich Village owned by Patrick Murphy, which Frank Wiborg bought from his daughter's father-in-law, presenting the deed to the newly married couple. From the very beginning of their marriage, they kept a full-time cook and a maid.

Gerald enlisted in the army in 1918, and was sent, as an officer, to the School of Aeronautics. He was eager to get into action, but, as was the case with F. Scott Fitzgerald, the First World War ended before he was able to join in the fighting. Sara, meanwhile, had in fairly quick succession three children, a daughter (Honoria), a son (Baoth), and another son (Patrick).

Feeling himself a flop at Mark Cross, where his father cut him very little slack, Gerald enrolled in a course of landscape architecture at Harvard, which he would drop out of before completing. (He and Sara shared a love for the visual arts.) Sara and the children followed him to Cambridge. Their social set in Cambridge-Boston included the poet Amy Lowell, the art collector Mrs. Isabella Gardner, the son and daughter-in-law of the philosopher William James, and the painter John Singer Sargent. Wherever they might find themselves, the Murphys were part of the in-crowd. "I would like to know those people," the then-young poet Archibald MacLeish said of them long before he became their friend. "They look so well laundered."

Gerald and Sara Murphy were, by instinct, avant-garde, socially and artistically. They were well in advance of their time on the subject of race, taking an early interest in black folk music and jazz. They welcomed the ultramodern in art and literature. This openness to the new made them feel that their own country was too restrictive for their tastes; the passing of Prohibition in 1919 certified for them the retrograde social condition of America. They began to think about leaving the country, which would have the added bonus of escaping their respective difficult families. They could only afford to think seriously about this, however, because Frank

Wiborg had decided to share his fortune among his three daughters before he died.

Gerald and Sara first went to England, and thence to Paris, where it didn't take them long to realize they had found a home. "Paris," Gerald said after being there a short while, "is bound to make a man either more or less American." The city seems to have made him both. With their charm as an entrée card, before long the Murphys were in the center of the artistic haut monde. Gerald devoted himself to painting, and soon he and Sara worked on painting the sets for the *Ballets Russes* version of Stravinsky's *Les Noces*.

"The Murphys were among the first Americans I ever met," Stravinsky would later say, "and they gave me the most agreeable impression of the United States." Picasso, sighting Gerald at the Opera of Paris, remarked: "There is American elegance." Picasso and his then-wife Olga became friends with the Murphys, and there was a rumor that Sara and Picasso had a brief love affair, the chief corroboration of which is Picasso's painting of a Sara-like figure naked but for the string of pearls Sarah herself habitually wore, even to the beach at their villa at Antibes.

The standard view of the Murphys is that they were an attractive couple who had little but their wealth as a calling card for their place among the avant-garde painters, writers, and musicians in Paris. In fact, they contributed to the efflorescence of the art of the twenties in a serious way. Gerald wrote the book and designed the sets for *Within the Quota*, a ballet produced by the *Les Ballets Suédois* for which Cole Porter, his friend from Yale, wrote the music, and Sara designed many of the costumes. Gerald's billboard-size painting, "Boatdeck," dominated the *Salon des Independents* show of 1922 and was a great *succès de scandal*.

Through their connection with the *Ballets Russes*, and through the early success of Gerald's paintings—both Leger and Picasso praised the latter—the Murphys also become great party-givers to the avant-garde. Excepting only James Joyce and Gertrude Stein, all the great names at one time or another showed up at the Murphys' parties: Diaghilev, Misia Sert, Leger, Darius Milhaud, Léonide Massine, Winnaretta de Polignac, Ernest Ansermet, Scofield Thayer, Tristan Tzara, Blaise Cendrars, Gilbert Seldes, Jean Cocteau, and many others. Man Ray photographed the Murphys at

Étienne de Beaumont's automotive ball, and, as Sylvia Beach noted, this "meant you were someone."

The Murphys' fame today derives chiefly from their connection with the American writers Archibald MacLeish, Dorothy Parker, Robert Benchley, Harry Crosby, Robert McAlmon, John Dos Passos, and, above all, F. Scott Fitzgerald and Ernest Hemingway. All these people befriended and at one time or another stayed with them. Fitzgerald and Hemingway put them, much modified, in their fiction. More than that, though, because of these two novelists, both so closely identified with the expatriate wing of the American Jazz Age, the Murphys are thought if not major, then certainly significant players in that most exhilarating of times.

Not long after buying and remodeling a stucco Moroccan-style villa in Antibes that they renamed Villa America, the Murphys took in Hemingway and Fitzgerald in times of crisis in each of their lives. When he first encountered the Murphys' lives, through the auspices of John Dos Passos and Donald Ogden Stewart, Hemingway was about to shed Hadley, his first wife. When Fitzgerald first met the Murphys, though his best writing was still ahead of him—*The Great Gatsby, Tender Is the Night*—he already had a drinking problem and his wife Zelda was well advanced on her way to the mental illness that afflicted her through the remainder of her life.

Both writers, according to the Murphys' excellent biographer Amanda Vaill, were at one point in love with Sara and envious of Gerald's marriage to her. Hemingway also suspected Gerald might be homosexual and wrote about the Murphys in *A Moveable Feast*, referring to them as "the rich," and treated them cruelly in that malicious book. He read parts of *The Sun Also Rises* to them, and, apropos of their praising the novel, noted: "If these bastards like it what is wrong with it?" Fitzgerald used Gerald and Sara in distorted form for his characters Dick and Nicole Diver in *Tender Is the Night*. (The Murphys, it needs to be said, were never anything but kind and generous to Hemingway and Fitzgerald, but such is the well-known ingratitude of novelists.) Philip Barry used them as characters in a play. Archibald MacLeish would also model characters in his play *J.B.* on them. Having writers for friends, obviously, is a perilous business.

A faded French aristocrat named the Prince de Faucigny-Lucinge claimed that the Murphys invented the Riviera as the great summer watering place. Certainly they made beach-going into an art. They would come down from Villa America, where they had no fewer than eight servants, with umbrellas and cocktail shakers, amusing beach hats, dogs, and their three beautiful children and lots of bright friends, and luxuriate in the sand along the Mediterranean. In their stylish opulence, they and such friends as happened to be with them—and they were seldom without friends—gave the phrase "the leisure class" palpable meaning.

The writer Donald Ogden Stewart referred to the Murphys as "the two people who had been our models for the Happy Life." None of this would have been possible, of course, without the cushioning of their money. But many people with lots of money don't find much happiness in life. The Murphys were never among the super-rich, yet, as Archibald MacLeish noted, "They always spent money as if they were, having a blithe contempt for money as such—a healthy conviction that money should be used for the purposes of life, the living of life, the defeat of illness and death." They were a stellar example of the charming rich.

Innumerable were the occasions when the Murphys helped out friends with money. Fitzgerald came to them to help him get his daughter through Vassar; Fernand Leger asked them for money to escape the Nazis; the novelist Dawn Powell, raising a child with serious mental problems, was another of the recipients of their generosity. When Dashiell Hammett, in poor health, needed to raise bail after being jailed for failing to turn in the names of Communists convicted of anti-government activity under the Smith Act, Gerald came up with $10,000 to help him out.

The Murphys bought and revamped houses and apartments with an impressive casualness. They seemed never to have lived anywhere that didn't provide beautiful views—of the Seine, of the Hudson, of Swiss Alps, of Mediterranean beaches, of lush countrysides. They dressed beautifully, not fashionably, but stylishly. They ate sublimely well, drank champagne with the same regularity that other people drink orange juice. They were unfailingly kind to and inventive at entertaining children. Charming, the Murphys were, in every way.

The curtain rang down on that immitigably happy life when in 1929 the Murphys' nine-year-old son Patrick was diagnosed with tuberculosis. Soon thereafter Gerald gave up his quietly but seriously flourishing career as a painter. Not long after, he underwent a Jungian analysis in Switzerland, where Patrick had earlier undergone treatment. He began confessing to friends—to Archibald MacLeish, to F. Scott Fitzgerald—that there had always been an emptiness at the center of his life, a detachment that made real friendship impossible. He claimed that he had no taste for life's realities—sadness, illness, death—that only the unreality he was able to create at Villa America and elsewhere in his life sustained him. "The *invented* part, for me, is what has meaning," he said.

Within two years the Murphys lost two sons: Baoth in 1935 to meningitis, Patrick in 1937 to tuberculosis. Sara went into a deep depression; Gerald took to wearing only black and gray for the rest of his days. They carried on, kept up the show, but now to their friends they became tragic figures. Gerald's painting had a revival, when the Dallas Museum of Modern Art did an exhibition of his work. When biographies of Hemingway and Fitzgerald began to be published, the Murphys came in for more publicity. They became part of the great mythos of the American expat generation of the 1920s.

After the death of their two sons, there was something a bit hollow about the Murphys' lives. As Sara wrote to Scott Fitzgerald: "I don't think the world is a very nice place—And all there seems to be left to do is to make the best of it while we are here, & be VERY grateful for one's friends—because they are the best there is, & make up for many another thing that is lacking."

Their surviving child, Honoria, gave the Murphys three grandchildren, for which they were grateful and on whom they lavished their generous attention. Sara did volunteer charity work. Gerald worked on a ballet with Richard Rodgers for which he received very little credit. Their biographer Amanda Vaill suggests that insufficiently repressed homosexuality was at the heart of Gerald's feeling of emptiness, but if he did have strong homosexual feelings he never, so far as is known, acted on them. Nor, so far as is known, did Sara ever have a love affair with Hemingway, who used to send her passionate letters. If Gerald and Sara tended to pull apart in later years, in the end they stayed together, each loyal to the other, each recognizing that it was only in combination, as a couple, as the eminently charming Murphys, that they were the extraordinary people they were.

Gerald Murphy died of intestinal cancer in 1964, at the age of seventy-six. Sara lived on, under a fog of dementia, until 1975, dying at ninety-two. After Gerald's death, Sara held a quietly elegant funeral party for a small number of remaining friends. Dawn Powell, who was among those invited, remarked that "it was a lesson in courage disguised as *taste*." To their last days, the Murphys never let down the side. They lived stylishly until the end. They were the Murphys, outwardly that most generous and charming of all charmed couples. What they were inwardly was nobody's business other than their own.

In 1962 a *New Yorker* writer named Calvin Tomkins wrote a lengthy profile, later published as a book, about the Murphys called *Living Well Is the Best Revenge*; they agreed to allow him to interview them for it, with the understanding that Gerald's paintings and the death of their sons would not be up for discussion. Tomkins' title, it is now evident, was a great misfit. The Murphys may have lived well, but there was no one against whom to take revenge for the great sadnesses visited upon them by the fates.

More than Hemingway, Picasso, or any of the other figures at the Murphys' Villa America, F. Scott Fitzgerald seemed to have the best shot at the charmed life. Handsome, talented, with a beautiful wife and early literary success, he appeared to be among the favorites of the gods. The representative figure in what came to be known as the Jazz Age, he is sometimes thought to have invented the phrase. When one thinks of Princeton, one thinks first of F. Scott Fitzgerald, even though he was an entirely uninterested student while there and left without a degree. The name Scott, given to so many young boys by parents swept away by Fitzgerald's allure—an allure built on the combination of talent allied to elegance—is another sign of his unending attraction to people who can never have met him yet took him, owing to his writing, for a man of the greatest charm.

Such has been the attraction of Fitzgerald's reputation as a figure of charm that it may well exceed his accomplishments as a writer, though those accomplishments were considerable. No one was thought more stylish than he. His literary style was imbued with charm; he wrote sentences of such lilting elegance that they seemed to heighten life and fill it with lovely possibilities in the way that only charm itself at its best can do.

In fact, F. Scott Fitzgerald's life was a great sad botch. He himself hadn't any doubt about it, and he said as much to his daughter Scottie, reporting his wish that he hadn't allowed so many distractions to get him off the track of serious literary production. (He also said it publicly in his one work of nonfiction, *The Crack-Up*.) But, owing to high and careless living, alcoholism, and social envy, he had gotten off that track. Snobbery, self-pity, and thwarted ambition, all to be sure attractively set out in his writing, were among the key themes in his life. A great chasm existed between the genuine elegance of his writing and the no less genuine squalor of his life.

Fitzgerald's alcoholism made him precisely the sort of guest you wouldn't want at your party. He and his Zelda's idea of a good bit of fun was to take everyone's watches and jewelry at a party and boil them in a can or pan over the stove. They would destroy furniture, ruin meals, insult other guests, get in punch-ups. Booze made them, the very reverse of charming, boorish in the extreme.

But for his alcoholism, but for his wife's insanity, but for his unrealistic nature, F. Scott Fitzgerald might have been a candidate for one of the most charming of American lives. He had an early success with his novel *This Side of Paradise*, he'd won the girl of his ardent dreams, and in later years, recalling the happiness all this brought him, he wrote: "I remember riding in a taxi one afternoon between very tall buildings under a mauve and rosy sky. I began to bawl because I had everything I wanted and knew I would never be so happy again."

Although he would write a better novel—a splendid novel, in fact, *The Great Gatsby*—he would never really be happy again. He felt in a permanent state of inferiority touching on masochism to such lesser writers as Ernest Hemingway and Edmund Wilson, both of whom put him down resoundingly after his death. He blew vast sums of money on stylish but finally empty frivolity. He went out to Hollywood in the hope of paying the expenses of private schools for his daughter and expensive mental institutions for his wife, but was too much the true artist to succeed there. "As soon as I feel I am writing to a cheap specification," he wrote, "my pen freezes and my talent vanishes over the hill." He did write the core of a brilliant but unfinished novel about Hollywood called *The Last Tycoon*.

In 1940 F. Scott Fitzgerald died, of a heart attack, his books out of print, feeling himself entirely out of luck, at the age of forty-four. In the end his unedifying life was preponderantly, incontestably, immitigably sad and much closer to damned than charmed. Yet he is important to the story of charm, at least in its American version, because he so yearned for the elegant, the orderly, the charmed life, and fell so sadly far short of it.

Are there any truly charmed lives? Are there people who go through all their days unmarked by life's darker vicissitudes: mistaken marriages, children who don't turn out, the death of loved ones, untimely and possibly painful deaths of their own by an arbitrary disease or (more arbitrary still) accidents?

F. Scott Fitzgerald wrote that "the test of a first-rate intelligence is the ability to hold two opposed ideas in the mind at the same time, and still retain the ability to function." When it comes to charmed lives, the way this might work is to hope for such a life for oneself and for one's children, all the while understanding that its attainment isn't very likely.

And yet charming people continue to turn up, some to flourish. As for charm itself, it remains the heightened pleasure that a small number of socially gifted people, of both sexes and differing social classes, bestow upon the rest of us, convincing us, while in the company of those with this gift, that the world, despite much evidence to the contrary, is still a delight-filled, gorgeous, altogether splendid place.

CHAPTER VII

Charming Rogues

CONSIDER THE CHARMING ROGUE. THE CHARMING ROGUE NEVER EXPENDS HIS charm without a motive; he puts his charm to gainful purposes; he has agendas, generally hidden. In the movies, the charming rogue has sometimes been played by Clark Gable, sometimes by Errol Flynn, more recently to comic effect by George Clooney. In the movies of the 1930s and '40s, George Saunders and Adolphe Menjou and George Macready played variants on the charming rogue, the well-spoken backguard, with the accent falling on the second word. Dashing, risk-taking, immensely confident, the charming rogue is sometimes a con man, often a seducer, always an operator.

I have encountered a few charming rogues in my life, but the first was a then-twenty-year-old named Jack Libby. His mother and mine grew up together on Chicago's west side, and remained friends. Jack was dark, nice looking, a gambler, a man with a good laugh. At the University of Illinois, where he was a business major, he began each autumn semester in September by having a fraternity brother hide his books and promise not to return them until November. He had a bookie in Urbana. Women with a taste for adventure were drawn to him.

Easily bored, Jack was in need of regular action. We used to play in poker games together, on one occasion in a shed in the old Fulton Street produce market in Chicago with several suspicious and mildly menacing characters around the table. He once suggested that we go in partnership in our respective fraternities in getting together bets against the University of Illinois basketball team for an important upcoming game with Iowa.

We gave a slightly false point spread, took Iowa, then laid all these bets off, betting on Illinois with the true point spread with Jack's bookie in Urbana. The hope here was to get in between the false and the true point spread. Between us, we got up roughly $500 in bets—a significant sum in those days—which Jack duly laid off. Iowa won, but by too many points for us to collect both ways, a sum of $1,000, which was the plan and would have constituted a fine little coup. But everyone in both fraternities thought we won, and at Jack's fraternity they threw him in the shower with his clothes on.

We lost touch. I had heard that Jack had married a girl from Memphis and moved down there. His wife's family supposedly had a large and successful furniture store, but, the report was, that was too conventional and dull for Jack, so he started a borax operation of some kind, selling home improvements through a bank of phones in a basement—a true boiler-room operation. Eight or so years later, on a flight from Little Rock, Arkansas, to Chicago that stopped in Memphis, I called him. When he asked me what I was doing, I said that I was working for the government as the director of the anti-Poverty Program in Little Rock. "I'm working for the government, too," he said. "They have a $100,000 lien on my business." That was the last I heard of him. Life was never dull around Jack, and I hope over the years he found enough escapades to keep boredom at bay.

Some charming rogues operate on a larger scale than others. The greatest charming rogue of all time, beyond doubt, was the Athenian Alcibiades (c.450–404 BC). His handsomeness was legendary; he was said to look as one might imagine Achilles to have looked. He had a lisp, but even this impediment was thought attractive, and many contemporaries even tried to imitate it. His lineage was aristocratic. When his father died at the battle of Coronea (447 BC), Pericles, the greatest of Athenian leaders, and his brother, Ariphron, became Alcibiades' guardians. Nothing of Pericles' principled leadership, high virtue, or ascetic habits rubbed off on Alcibiades—another case in which nature once again soundly drubbed nurture.

Alcibiades' teacher was Socrates, who recognized his extraordinary qualities—and to whom Alcibiades offered himself physically, or so it is recorded in Plato's *Symposium*. Here, too, Alcibiades, who much admired

Socrates, came through uninfluenced by the great philosopher's wisdom. Ambitious, vain, keen for glory, with time out only for roistering and seduction, he was always in business exclusively for himself.

No matter how egregious Alcibiades' behavior, the people of Athens seem never to have grown tired of him. "As a boy, as a youth, as a man," his biographer E. F. Benson writes of him, "he had a unique charm and distinction which continually earned him forgiveness for the most outrageous escapades. Athens always pardoned him and yearned for him even when he had brought on her storms of ruin and disaster." Benson adds: "Vicious, insolent, adorable, detestable, brilliant and fickle, with the face and body of a god and the wit of Aristophanes, he was the very incarnation of the spirit of Athens . . . The whole town was in love with him. Never had Athens seen a boy of such amazing beauty. He had wit and charm, high breeding (for all his escapades) and wealth, and Athens was mad about him, and did her utmost, with conspicuous success, to spoil him."

Alcibiades was known for erratic acts of behavior: showing off for companions, boxing the ears of a dignified citizen (his future father-in-law, as it happened), cutting off the tail of his own large dog. He attracted and throve on attention. He married well, acquiring a large dowry, which didn't stop him from keeping regular company with courtesans and roisterers. He spent lavishly. He sent seven chariots to the Olympic games, and won three of the top four prizes. Euripides and Thucydides differ about whether he won first, second, and third, or first, second, and fourth prize in the chariot race, an unprecedented result in either case.

While still young, Alcibiades fought in the battle of Potidaea, where he was wounded, and Socrates, fighting by his side, is said to have saved his life. His military record, along with his personal wealth and noble birth, eased his way into the always chancy political life of Athens. He had great oratorical skills, with, as Plutarch notes, "the highest capacity for inventing, for discerning what was the right thing to be said for any purpose, and on any occasion; but aiming not only at saying what was required, but also saying it well, in respect, that is, of words and phrases." Nor, one might add, was he ever inconvenienced by the need to adhere to true sentiment or made in the least hesitant by the pull of conscience.

Alcibiades was envious of one thing only—glory won by others, for he wanted it all for himself. Nicias, an older general, said to have ended the war with Sparta through his statesmanship, was a particular target for Alcibiades' envy. Through his deceptions, he was able to put down Nicias, depriving him of the credit he had earned through what was known as the Peace of Nicias, and in effect restarting the war of the Peloponnesus, with himself now one of the leading Athenian generals.

Dressed extravagantly in long purple robes, Alcibiades had the figure of Cupid holding aloft a thunderbolt in his hand emblazoned on his shield, ate heartily, drank copiously, and went in for dissolution in a serious way and quite without regard for public opinion. Aristophanes noted of the Athenians reaction to him: "They love, and hate, and cannot do without him." Plutarch filled this out when he wrote: "The truth is, [Alcibiades'] liberalities, his public shows, and other munificence to the people, which were such as nothing could exceed; and the glory of his ancestors, the force of his eloquence, the grace of his person, his strength of body, joined with his great courage and knowledge in military affairs prevailed upon the Athenians to endure patiently his excesses, to indulge his faults, attributing them to youth and good nature."

Alcibiades' great moment arrived when he persuaded the Athenian assembly of the need for attacking Sicily and annexing it to the island empire that Athens had already established through its powerful navy. Before he was to set sail with his expedition for Sicily, a number of religious statues, called herms, had been defaced, and witnesses came forth to blame it on a drunken Alcibiades and his friends, who were also said to have mocked the religious rites known as the Eleusinian mysteries. Alcibiades denied having anything to do with either charge, and demanded to stand trial before the Sicilian expedition, but was ordered to sail away first and await trial on his return. While he was gone, his enemies at Athens stirred up sufficient talk against him so that he was recalled from Sicily to stand trial. Sensing the game was up, even though he was probably innocent, Alcibiades escaped to Thurii on the Tarentine Gulf and thence to Argos.

One of the great "What If's?" of history asks what if Alcibiades had been allowed to pursue aggressively the campaign against Sicily, which, before his hurried departure, appeared to be on the brink of success? Would it have brought about victory and Athenian supremacy for decades to come? Instead his fellow general, Nicias, acting too cautiously, was routed, and at great cost to the Athenians. A debacle ensued in which Athens lost much the better part of its naval and land forces, and would never regain its former power.

Meanwhile Alcibiades, always the self-starter, contacted the Spartans and offered them his services. These turned out to be considerable. He instructed them to send a force to Sicily to help defeat the Athenians there; he also advised them to continue the war against a now much weakened Athens, and to fortify the lands around Athens, in the hope of starving out the city. Sound advice—and all of it directed against his own people.

While in Sparta, Alciabides Spartanized himself. Cutting his hair, eating coarse Spartan food, bathing in cold water, he went native. "At Sparta," Plutarch writes, "he was devoted to athletic exercises, was frugal and reserved; in Ionia, luxurious, gay, and indolent; in Thrace, always drinking; in Thessaly, ever on horseback; and when he lived with Tissaphernes [the powerful Persian satrap] he exceeded the Persians themselves in magnificence and pomp." He was, in other words, willing to do whatever the situation in which he found himself required. Like the chameleon, he was able, as Plutarch says, to turn himself into every color but white.

Alcibiades might have gone on to become a great Spartan general, but for a little contretemps. He seems to have made pregnant the wife of the Spartan King Agis. He later claimed to have done this so that his would be the true line of Spartan kings. Since Agis had been away from home for ten months, that the child could not be his allowed of no doubt. When it was reported to Agis that his wife's child was fathered by Alcibiades, the latter knew he had overstayed his welcome in Sparta. Agis and other leading figures in Sparta, who had become envious of his reputation for military victories, put out orders that Alcibiades be assassinated.

This sent Alcibiades directly into the arms of the powerful Persian satrap Tissaphernes. He served as an influential adviser to the Persians, instructing them on how to gain dominance over the Athenians and Spartans both, by playing one off the other. Plutarch puts it neatly:

For this barbarian, not being himself sincere, but a lover of guile and wickedness, admired his [Alcibiades'] address and wonderful subtlety. And, indeed, the charm of daily intercourse with him was more than any character could resist or any disposition escape. Even those who feared and envied him could not but take delight and have a sort of kindness for him, when they saw him and were in his company.

Athenians, Spartans, Persians, Alcibiades charmed them all, and to the highest power.

Even in the most enviable of situations, it was not in Alcibiades' nature to rest content for long. Contentment is not in the armory of emotions or conditions of the charming rogue. To make a complex story simple, Alcibiades yearned to return to Athens, and devised a way to do so by pitting the Persians against the Spartans. Once returned to Athens, where a strong faction, so taken with his genius, wanted him to rule as tyrant, he helped the city-state recoup much of its lost empire. He made, however, too many enemies in Athens, in Sparta, among Persians. E. F. Benson notes: "His own beauty and charm were always his greatest enemies, for up to the end his most hideous transgressions of the codes of loyalty and honor were always forgiven him." That end now had come.

E. F. Benson set his epitaph: "Indeed, the dictum of Archestratus was true, that while Greece could not stand more than one Alcibiades, Athens would have lacked the complete incarnation of her splendor and her shame without him, there must needs have been one Alcibiades, and he Athenian."

In the end Alcibiades went off alone—in the company of a mistress, of course—to Bithynia, eventually to retire to a small village in Phrygia. The Spartans had put a hit order out on him, assigning it to the Persian satrap Pharnabazus. Those assigned to murder him, it is said, hadn't the courage to face him, and so set afire the house in which he was living. Alcibiades was naked, clutching his clothes, departing the house, sword in hand, when they brought him down with arrows and darts. A conflicting story has him murdered in the same manner by the brothers of a lady of noble family whom he had seduced. I prefer this latter story, on the basis of no historical fact whatsoever, because death brought on as a result of heedless seduction seems a more appropriate way for a charming rogue to meet his end than at the hands of an enemy.

The boy Giacomo Casanova did not at birth seem a strong candidate for a prominent place in the gallery of charming rogues. The grandson of a cobbler, the child of two traveling actors, he was a puny child, born with an unlabeled illness that caused him to hemorrhage from the nose from the age of ten years old or so. His father died young, his mother was inattentive; he was raised by a grandmother and educated by priests. Bright enough, he studied for the priesthood himself, and actually for a time became a friar, a strange occupational choice for a man who was to become one of the world's most famous seducers of women.

Casanova soon enough grew wary of the ecclesiastical life, though in his young manhood it gave him entrée, as a tutor, into the homes of the Italian nobility. With his learning, his theatrical manner of presenting himself, his sense of his own higher nobility—a nobility above that of mere family connection—he set out to seek pleasure by the novel method of bestowing it. His weapons here were beautiful manners, a display of learning, an ability to blend perfectly into his surroundings, sparkling conversation—in a word, charm. In Naples, Rome, Padua, Venice, the still-adolescent friar everywhere ingratiates, insinuating himself into the best society, where women especially seem to enjoy his boyish company.

Peripeteia, reversal of fortune, came when Giacomo, after dinner one night at the home of his patron at the time, an elderly Venetian senator named Malipiero, as the old man is napping off, begins fondling Malipiero's mistress. The older man wakes, discovers the two at play, begins beating on Giacomo with his cane, instructs him never to return to his palace again. Not long after, Casanova gives up his ecclesiastical career.

He had earlier learned to play the violin, and now falls back on his skill as a violinist to earn his keep. One night, working in an orchestra hired to play at a wedding, he encounters another rich Venetian senator, whom he follows home, where the senator undergoes a stroke. Giacomo stays the night with him, nurses him, and when he returns to health, the senator, a man named Bragadin, all but adopts him. Peripeteia is almost a game with Casanova; he goes from out the frying pan into the beds of interesting women, back into the frying pan. He also begins to sense that the standard rules of life do not apply to him.

Casanova will drift into and out of jobs—musician, soldier, actor—but his main work will be the seduction of women. His is seduction, however, with a difference. He allows women to join him in the act of seduction, making known only his availability. In his memoirs, as a boy learning Latin he notes the peculiarity that the word for vagina (*cunnus*) is masculine while the word for penis (*mentula*) is feminine. From this he deduces, a lifelong lesson, that the slave always takes the name of the master.

A *casanova* has come to mean a charmer who is master of the art of seducing women. Yet Giacomo Casanova was the reverse of the conventional seducer. He was, for one, the least misogynist of men as seducers not infrequently are. "The professional seducer," he writes in his memoirs, ". . . is an abominable man, essentially the enemy of the person on whom he has designs. He is a true criminal who, if he has the qualities required to seduce, makes himself unworthy of them by abusing them to make a woman unhappy." Casanova's own modus operandi was the direct opposite. He let women seduce him. He arranged this by making plain how deeply infatuated he was with any woman with whom he sought intimacy. He didn't have to invent his infatuations; they were real. To him intimacy with a woman was truly ecstasy. He writes that, though he realizes he is a voluptuary, until the age of sixty "I continued to be the dupe of women."

"Giacomo cannot help being sincerely infatuated by each woman he desires," writes Lydia Flem in *Casanova, The Man Who Really Loved Women*. "Malice is never involved. Love intrigues him; for him love is neither philandering nor vanity. It is a kind of madness, an incurable disease." When the love between Casanova and his various women ends, the break is always clean; no hard feelings but gratitude on both sides.

The only near contemporary of whom something similar seems to have been true is George Balanchine, the world's last great choreographer, who married five times and had many love affairs with his dancers. Women who took up with Balanchine seemed to understand that he took up with them, as in some ways did Pablo Picasso with his wives and lovers, as muses, or stimulants to his art. As lovers, these women appeared to be glad to have been of service. Giacomo Casanova, though, had no specific art to offer, apart from that of giving and receiving pleasure, and this seems to have been more than sufficient.

Over the span of his memoirs, Casanova recounts making love to, among many others, two sisters (simultaneously), a mother and daughter, noblewomen (both French and Italian), a nun, and a false castrato posing as a man with whom he later learns he has had an illegitimate son. He underwent several bouts of venereal disease, which he treated, successfully, with a six-week diet of nitrate water. Only orgies, with their indiscriminateness, put him off. "His life," Lydia Flem writes, "is a race of desire, a conjuration, an obstinate way of rejecting anything that prevents enjoyment. He has a stubborn taste for happiness, and amusement and lightness are his favorite weapons."

Of what did Giacomo Casanova's charm consist? He was a brilliant conversationalist, no doubt a superior sexual athlete, but neither an Adonis of handsomeness nor someone who held out the promise of marriage, security, or even fidelity in his relations with women. He lived most fully in the present—the only tense he knew. He also seems to have known when to quit, to get out of the game, lest he be judged a sad roué, a debauched old lecher. At the age of sixty-four he retired from the boudoir and began to write his memoirs—he would die at seventy-three—which allowed him to recount, to relive for himself and anyone else interested, the loves of his life, a work impressively free of the note of regret.

Giacomo Casanova's was the charm of freedom, holding out the promise to live, however briefly, outside the constraints of custom, proprieties, morality itself. His was the promise of living and loving wholly in accord with one's true nature, in the honest delight of sensual pleasure. The promise was fullfilled for him and for the countless women on whom he expended his apparently inexhaustible charm.

A different sort of charming rogue was Lord Byron, operating on a smaller canvas than Alcibiades and consequently of greatly lesser historical significance, even though his name is more widely known. Byron's charm, like Casanova's, was mostly in the realm of sexual conquest, though not there alone. Nearly everyone who met him was taken by him, including his many servants, a refutation of Hegel's claim that no man is a hero to his valet. Part of his attraction had to do with his fame, which began with the publication of his poem *Childe Harold* (first published in 1812, when he was twenty-four), based on his travels to Turkey and other then exotic climes. His dashing good looks didn't hurt. His reputation was summed up by one of his many lovers, Caroline Lamb, who called him "bad, mad, and dangerous to know."

For those who believe there is no such thing as a bad boy, only bad and sad circumstances, the saddest of all such circumstances being having wretched parents, George Gordon Byron qualifies nicely. His father was, in the old-fashioned phrase, a blackguard, his mother absurd. Captain Byron married her for her money, squandered it, and disappeared. Debt was a permanent condition for the family, as it would be for Byron throughout his extravagantly lived life. Not that he let financial problems much disturb him. Along with being born to hopeless parents, Byron came into the world with a deformed foot, owing to a withered calf muscle in his right leg. Achilles had his heel, but it didn't render him lame, as did Byron's foot. Byron took much abuse during his early school years because his deformed foot caused him noticeably to limp. The first girl he was attracted to, Mary Chaworth, when asked by her maid whether she returned his love, replied: "Why do you think I could feel anything for that lame boy?" Byron overheard the remark, and was devastated by it. In later years he would take revenge for it on several women, including a by-then-married Mary Chaworth, whom he subsequently seduced.

George Gordon Byron only became a lord because of the early death of a cousin ahead of him in line of succession for the title. He was to the manner, if not quite the manor, born, lordly in his spending, his style, above all his grandiose sense of himself. His family was very far from the first line of English aristocrats, but you could not tell it by him. Before his own careening career brought the word into being, he was never less than Byronic, with all that implies of heedless sexual conquest, contemptuous grandeur, and the inability to put anyone's interest and feelings before his own.

Rake, roué, the very model of the Regency buck, Lord Byron was, in the tradition of the charming rogue, quite without a conscience. ("I have a conscience," he said, "although the world gives me no credit for it; I am now repenting, not the few sins I have committed, but of the many I have not committed.") Freudians might say that this came about because he grew up without a father, the source, they like to think, of the super-ego. Byron would have had a good laugh at the notion of the superego, though he might have bought the Freudian emphasis on the centrality of sex in the human psychic economy. He may have had a premonition of his own early demise, for he lived, like most charming rogues, exclusively in and for the moment. In Venice, hearing a church bell, he told his friend Percy Bysshe Shelley that the ringing bell reminded him of the call of conscience. "We obey it like madmen," he said, "without knowing why, then the sun sets. The bell stops. It is the night of death."

A highly sexual being, Lord Byron—nor, in the realm of sex, a highly discriminating one. He didn't have to be. Once his fame was established, women came after him. In fashionable society, being bonked by Byron was up there with being painted by Gainsborough. He did whatever his fancy struck him to do—sodomy, incest, Roman rent boys, Piccadilly trollops—with whomever happened to be available, for free or for hire. Frederic Raphael, his most penetrating biographer, refers to Byron as "the most desired man in England, perhaps in the world . . . the catch of the century."

What did Byron, this most appealing of all men to women, look like? His contemporary, Edward John Trelawny, encountering Byron in Italy in 1822, wrote:

In external appearance Byron realized that idealized standard with which imagination adorns genius. He was in the prime of life; thirty-four; of middle height, five feet eight and a half inches; regular features without a stain or furrow on his pallid skin, his shoulders broad, chest open, body and limbs finely proportioned. His small highly finished head and curly hair had an airy and graceful appearance from the massiveness and length of his throat; you saw his genius in his eyes and lips. In short, Nature could have done little more than she had done for him, both in outward form and in the inward spirit she had given to animate it.

Trelawny then goes on to mention Byron's deformed foot: "But all these rare gifts to his jaundiced imagination only served to make his one personal defect [his lameness] the more apparent, as a flaw is magnified in a diamond when polished; and he brooded over that blemish, as sensitive minds will brood until they magnifiy a wart into wen." This same flaw, Trelawny felt, "helped to make him skeptical, cynical, and savage."

No man seemed freer than Byron. He treated his creditors as if they were fortunate to hold his debts. His verbal cruelty was famous; whatever was on his lung was on his tongue. Contemning children, he claimed to approve Herod's plan to massacre them. He had no remorse about hurting feelings; a clever jibe was worth the pain it caused. Heterodoxy was his orthodoxy. As with all charming rogues, boredom was always a problem for him. He was also visited by melancholy, which turned out to be an attraction for women, so many of whom thought they had the where-withal that could relieve it for him.

Women may have been stimulated by his hauteur, his impertinence, his disregard of all conventions while still enjoying his aristocratic social privileges. His good looks with the touch of vulnerability about him lent by his limp didn't hurt. His contempt for women may have stimulated them even further. His reputation preceded him—in neon and with trumpet accompaniment. He once told Shelley that he believed women had neither souls nor rights. Because of this view, he felt not the least compunction about being utterly disloyal to them.

For all his cool distance, Byron prided himself on his desirability. He courted adoration through the well-lubricated instrument of his charm. "He was endowed with a seductive charm," as Frederic Raphael notes, and he enjoyed exercising it. He apparently had no close friends but lots of jolly companions. The biggest mistake women could make was to attempt sustained intimacy with him, leading to a permanent connection. He never saw the point of repaying pleasure in the coin of loyalty.

Nor—no surprise here—was he without vanity. He worried about running to fat, and went on near-starvation diets, swam vast distances, including on one occasion the Hellespont. He dressed all in black. A receding hairline was another worry. He was exceptionally conscious of youth passing away. He went in for costumes, and one of his best is on display in the famous portrait Thomas Phillips painted of him in Greek headdress. When he went to Greece, near the end of his life, to help the Greeks liberate themselves from the Turks, he acquired a helmet modeled on fifth-century Greek battle gear. He was always playing to an audience, and the role he played was that of Lord Byron.

The one time he stepped out of character, he did so to marry Annabella Milbanke, the niece of Lady Melbourne and herself heiress to a large fortune. He claimed to yearn for routine and respectability, a yearning that turned out to be little more than a passing whim. He was dreadful in the role of husband, impatient, disappointing, naturally unfaithful. He already had a daughter with his half-sister Augusta—a subject of great scandal in the drawing rooms of London—and soon he had another with his wife. He made pregnant a third young woman, Clair Clairmont, who had the impertinence to follow him to Italy, wanting to be in his company. All three of his children were daughters—seducers, in cosmic retribution, are often the fathers of multiple daughters—none would know his affection for extended periods.

Between his whoring and roistering, his travel and lavish spending—on coaches, foreign villas and palazzos, on small ships, and more—the wonder is that he got as much work done as he did. According to Edward Trelawny, he thought up rhymes for his poetry during afternoon horseback rides, and, after his usual social round, set them to paper late into the night. Don Juan, the poem for which he is best remembered, added to the éclat of his delicious scandalousness. When the wife of the radical journalist Leigh Hunt was asked about Byron's morals, she said that this was the first she had heard of them.

Perhaps the best way to know Byron is through his letters, though nearly everything he wrote was touched by autobiography. His memoirs were destroyed by his publisher John Murray on the grounds that they were too salacious—an act itself comprising one of the great literary losses and publishing scandals of all time. He is remembered as a poet, though he now seems less than a first-class one—the Romantic who really wasn't a Romantic and who himself had no taste for the poetry of Wordsworth, Coleridge, or Keats. Byron's life overshadowed his poetry; always did, always will. He preferred not to be treated as a writer, Trelawny reports, but instead as a lord and man of fashion.

He died young, as befits an Adonis, at thirty-four, in Greece, at Misso-longhi. He didn't die fighting for Greek independence, as he had hoped, but owing to illness. The cause of death was supposedly urima, but the killer was in fact that famous serial killer, nineteenth-century medicine, for in the attempt to lower his fever Byron was bled and purged by physicians until weakened to the point of death and then beyond. His heart is buried in Greece, his body in England, though not in Westminster Abbey, with the great English poets, for he was thought too scandalous to qualify for official enshrinement, which seems only fitting for the most charming rogue of the nineteenth century.

Vastly less well-known than Alcibiades, Casanova, or Lord Byron, another figure in the charming rogue's gallery, perhaps one off in one of its quieter rooms, was Morton Fullerton, a man whose slight fame resides in the fact that he apparently gave sexual satisfaction to the novelist Edith Wharton, though she appears not to have done the same for him. Fullerton was what, in another time, was called a ladies man. Born a New Englander in 1865, a contemporary of George Santayana's at Harvard, as a young man Fullerton expatriated himself and landed a job as the second correspondent in Paris for the London *Times*. He became a friend to Henry James, whom some say used Fullerton as a model for the character Merton Denscher, the journalist who, with his lover Kate Croy, attempts to do Milly Theale out of her fortune in James' novel *The Wings of the Dove*. Edith Wharton put a Fullerton-like character in her novel *The Reef*, though she chose not to mention him in her memoir *A Backward Glance*. Fullerton thought himself the attractive young man Santayana called Mario in *The Last Puritan*, though he was mistaken in this.

A smallish man, five feet six inches, with blue eyes and a serious mustache, well turned out, Morton Fullerton was attractive to women. His biographer, Marion Mainwaring, writes of him: "He had a strong heart, serviceable lungs in spite of lifelong smoking, a tricky gallbladder, an agile, catholic penis; he had a soft voice and charm." About the precision of Miss Mainwaring's two adjectives before the word *penis*, one is left uncertain, but of Fullerton's charm everyone seems to have agreed. Henry James wrote to him: "You bear I won't say a charmed but certainly a charming life."

Fullerton was, like Alcibiades and Lord Byron, happily bisexual. (Truly charming rogues apparently want to seduce everyone.) His susceptibility to male beauty is said to have been as great as that to feminine beauty. He proposed marriage to several women; he had an illegitimate daughter. One of his many lady friends blackmailed him. He no sooner moved a woman into his lodgings, or moved into hers, than he was on the hunt for another. At one point between the wars he kept a room at the Elysee Hotel used exclusively for trysts, with men and with women.

Yet for all his charm—or might it be because of his great charm—Morton Fullerton was not, as the world reckons it, a success. He never rose to be the *Times'* first correspondent in Paris, a job of great importance, nearly, in its potential influence, on the level of the English ambassador. As a journalist, the judgment against him was that he was unexceptional. He wrote a book called *Problems of Power* that attracted the praise of Theodore Roosevelt, and allowed him to set up for a time as an expert in European politics. He had a column in *Le Figaro,* which gave him a certain voice in French affairs. In the end, though, it all came to nothing.

The near full-time distractions of Fullerton's sexual life worked against the smooth ascent of a successful career. Was he what today in a more therapeutic-minded time we should call a sex addict? His biographer claimed that "his easy enjoyment of pleasure and obvious talent for giving pleasure, undifferentiated as to men or women, were less about love, or even sex, than about control." And yet his sexual prowess, combined with his charm, got him a long way further than his innate talent alone figured to have done.

"As an unusually beautiful youth he found that he could exert influence over older, well-to-do important men who took him to Europe, took him to Greece and Egypt, found him a professional position beyond his qualifications," Marion Mainwaring writes. Fullerton's charm opened many doors, and subsequently turned back many sheets, but he couldn't bring to fruition the opportunities his charm presented to him. In a letter to Edith Wharton, Henry James wrote that news of Fullerton's being down on his luck caused him "quite a hideous little pang, leaving one afresh as it does, bang up against that exquisite art in him of not bringing it off to which his treasure of experience and intelligence, of accomplishment, talent, ambition, charm, everything, so inimitably contributes."

Fullerton was an operator with no power of calculation. He alienated his employers on the *Times* through his presumption. He could doubtless have married the wealthy Edith Wharton, who was besotted with him, after her divorce from her husband Teddy, which would have put an end to all his financial troubles, but chose not to do so. When he did marry, the marriage lasted a year. He always went either too far or not far enough.

Charming rogues do best, perhaps, to die young. Morton Fullerton lived too long, nearly to the age of eighty-seven. He remained in Paris through the Nazi occupation during World War Two, with a woman, of course, a Mme Pouget, on short rations and insufficient fuel. Strongly anti-German during World War One, in World War Two he befriended Frenchmen friendly toward Hitler, which made his existence after the liberation of Paris precarious. With age he grew shabby. Leon Edel, doing research for his biography of Henry James, called on Fullerton, and was given "something of a shock to see this still handsome old man who had always been . . . a fashion plate, dressed in shabby clothes, and those fine mustaches now ragged and unkempt, his eyes bleary. . . But he was charming and melancholy; the charm was always there . . . ." Shabbiness and all, according to his cousin Hugh Fullerton, "even to the last he had charm for women."

Charm of Fullerton's kind wears thin. Seductions are not medals, lovers achievements. Men and women living on charm alone are soon enough forgotten. Not long before his death in 1952, poor Morton Fullerton learned with chagrin that his old college classmate George Santayana had left him out of his memoirs.

Continuing in diminuendo mode in this gallery of charming rogues, we come to Bruce Chatwin. To be in Chatwin's company was apparently to come instantly under his spell. "He was amazing to look at," wrote Susan Sontag. "There are few people in this world who have the kind of looks which enchant and enthrall. Your stomach just drops to your knees, your heart skips a beat, you're not prepared for it. I saw it in Jack Kennedy. And Bruce had it. It isn't just beauty, it's a glow, something in the eyes. And it works on both sexes." The writer Gregor von Rezzori called Bruce Chatwin "the Golden Boy."

The testimonials to the magic of his looks and personality pile up. Many are captured in Nicholas Shakespeare's biography of Bruce Chatwin. "His style was to be the beautiful soft child-boy who's not quite real, like a boy in an English school whom others have a crush on," noted the movie director James Ivory. "He was like that and he stayed like that. He was a Rupert Brooke." Salman Rushdie claimed that Chatwin was "so colossally funny you'd be on the floor with pain. When his stories hit their stroke, they could simply destroy you." A woman named Nin Dutton with whom over four days Chatwin drove across Australia reports that he "never stopped talking, and he was never boring ever, ever." The English journalist Shirley Conran compared Chatwin's charm on first meeting to being overcome by perfume, "a wonderful cloud of Miss Dior. I reeled away, drunk on it."

The son of a provincial lawyer, Bruce Chatwin as a child was the family entertainer. As mimic, storyteller, boy comedian, he early knew how to command attention. The only thing at school that much interested him was acting. He was throughout his life attracted to the exotic: in objects, in travel, in people. He became more than a bit of an exotic himself. Because he was undecided on a career, his father discouraged his applying to Oxford. With his easy charm and devastating good looks—blond, six foot tall, long-limbed, with perfect features, and with a dazzling smile—he didn't require diplomas and degrees to make his way through the world.

At eighteen, Chatwin talked his way into a job in London at Sotheby's, the auctioneers of artworks and antiquities. He began at a lowly place in the Furniture in the Works of Art Department, but soon rose up from there to be one of the company's key figures, especially when it came to convincing the rich to turn their collections over to Sotheby's for resale by auction. Some said his good looks were a lure to bring in the business of wealthy homosexual collectors. A colleague at Sotheby's named David Nash claimed that the auction house was the central experience in Chatwin's life. His work there provided him with an aesthetic education, allowed him foreign travel in search of antiquities, and introduced him to a circle of rich young people, among them his wife Elizabeth Chanler, an American with serious money on both sides of her family.

Elizabeth Chatwin knew her husband had had homosexual affairs, but didn't let it stop her from marrying the immensely attractive young Bruce Chatwin. None of his friends thought Bruce would ever marry. Elizabeth's family money gave him room to negotiate his life without the immediate compulsion of having to earn a living. Once married he took time off to study archaeology at the University of Edinburgh, to travel (often without his wife), to search out antiquities and objects d'art in Afghanistan, and cultivate his interest in exotic tribes in Africa and elsewhere.

Wherever Bruce Chatwin went, his charm was his passport. "Think of the word 'charming,'" said Miranda Rothschild, the sister of the banker Jacob Rothschild. "Think of the word 'seduction.' Think of seduction as a driving force to conquer society . . . [Bruce's] out to seduce everybody, it doesn't matter if you are male, female, an ocelot or a tea cosy." Miranda Rothschild was in a position to know, for Chatwin had seduced her, or perhaps she him; it's a bit unclear. He was, she claimed, a disappointing lover. Others, men and women, claimed similar disappointment in his prowess in this line. Might it be that the great narcissists, of whom Bruce Chatwin appears to have been one, finally love only themselves?

Shirley Conran held:

A lot of people were in love with Bruce, and I'm sorry for all of them. I saw the misery it brought. We have all loved people and left them, but when Bruce danced on to the next he had the ability to leave them feeling empty and bereft in a way I doubt they ever recovered from . . . [Chatwin was the reverse, in this respect, of Casanova and Balanchine.] He did not know himself and did not care to know himself too closely. He was like Ariel; in this world but not of it.

Charming his way across four continents, Chatwin turned himself into a travel writer in the mode of Robert Byron, author of *The Road to Oxiana*. He wrote books about Patagonia, the slave trade in West Africa, aboriginal Australians, and two novels. Once he determined on the writing life, he charmed his way into the good graces of the most prominent

English editor and publisher then in business, Tom Maschler at Jonathan Cape. "At present," he wrote to his friend Edith Welch, "I am focusing my attention and blandishments on Mr. Maschler." Like just about everyone else, Tom Maschler could not resist those blandishments. "I do remember being pretty taken with this young man," he recalled. "He had an extraordinary assurance and an integrity. I was sure I was dealing with someone very special." The books were all critically praised and did well commercially.

Kevin Volans, the South African composer, who was planning to write a musical score for Chatwin's book *Songlines*, met Chatwin to discuss it and was blown away by his charm. "I sat there like Scheherazade at the foot of his bed while he told me stories. There was literally nothing I wouldn't have done. I adored him. He was one of those people who did have the key to the world." Volans, too, became one of his lovers.

All the efforts of Bruce Chatwin's charm and talent had begun to pay off handsomely—fame, big money, the good opinion of peers—when he contracted AIDS. He fought off the knowledge of the disease for as long as he could, for he had so much to live for, and AIDS seemed so drastic a disappointment. But death, as is well-known, is wont to come when least wanted. Not even Bruce Chatwin could charm it away. He perished at the age of forty-nine.

Alcibiades, Casanova, Lord Byron, Morton Fullerton, Bruce Chatwin are only five names in the vast gallery of charming rogues. Some might wish to add Talleyrand, Frank Sinatra, Bill Clinton; others to argue that some among these men are more roguish than charming. (If there are or have been female rogue charmers, I do not know of them.) The main point is that roguishness is one of the forms that charm can take. Charm, the lives of the roguish charmers teach, has its dangers, sometimes to those upon whom it casts its spell, sometimes quite as much and even more to those who possess it.

CHAPTER VIII

Woman Charmers

THE CHARM OF WOMEN IS DIFFERENT FROM THAT OF MEN, WIDER RANGING, subtler, operating under different constraints and with a different sort of freedom. Men can be charming and sexy in roughly equal parts—Cary Grant, Gary Cooper, Errol Flynn, to name three movie stars, each different in the quality of his charmingness but all clearly thought sexy. Unclear whether women can in the same way be equally charming and sexy. In Marlene Dietrich, Sophia Loren, Rita Hayworth, the sexiness predominates over the charm, though in the instances of Barbara Stanwyck, Katherine Hepburn, and Myrna Loy, charm and sexiness are more equally distributed, in all three latter cases favoring charm over sexiness.

Unsexy men can, let us hope, also be charming. Sometimes, if I may speak for myself and my less-than-god-like confreres, it is all we have going for us. So, too, of course, can unsexy women be charming: the comedy writer Selma Diamond, the comedian Carol Burnett, the essayist Fran Lebowitz come to my unchivalrous mind. Julia Child could be charming with raw liver in her hands. With women, though, sex often obtrudes, blocking out charm. Men, being brutes, tend to give precedence to the erotic element over the element of charm in their assessment of women. Truly sexy women, for example, have little chance to become comedians; and if they attempt to do so, they must camouflage their natural sexual attractiveness behind the masks of their stage persona. Consider the careers of Lucille Ball, Irene Dunne, Tina Fey. Physically attractive women comedians have reported that, in the middle of their acts, men in the audience have been known to shout, "Take it off." Brutes, men, we're all brutes, as when she was young I never tired of instructing my beautiful granddaughter Annabelle.

A too-witty woman might also be a threat to a man. Wit, so often part of a man's charm, is less often considered charming in a woman. For some men, wit in a woman can be hazardous. Too witty a woman might be thought to laugh at a man at all the wrong times and in embarrassing places. From Pericles lover Aspasia through Lady Mary Wortley Montagu through Mesdames du Deffand, de Stael, and d'Épinay in eighteenth-century France through Margot Asquith, the Stephens sisters (Virginia Woolf and Vanessa Bell), and Alice Roosevelt Longworth, brilliant and subtle women have sometimes been center stage. Were they also charming? Some were, some weren't, but then more often than not a woman's charm has been more beckoning than witty, supporting than aggressive, alluring than challenging.

Tallulah Bankhead, the actress and international celebrity, was in some ways charming, though stories about her are perhaps more charming than she was herself, as they say, in person. In a characteristic anecdote, Tallulah returns to her hometown of Montgomery, Alabama, to visit her sister Eugenia. One night during her stay she is asked to babysit her sister's two notoriously ill-behaved sons, boys of twelve and eleven. She is instructed not to mind what the boys do, apart from setting fire to the place, because they have been so long out of control that there is no hope of disciplining them now. When Eugenia and her husband return home around 10:00 p.m., to their astonishment they discover the house in perfect order and the boys both asleep. When they asked Tallulah how she accomplished this, she, in her husky voice, answers: "Not really a problem, dahlings. I taught the little devils a new game that they seem to have taken to straightaway." When they ask her what the game is, Tallulah replies, "It's called masturbation, dahlings."

Whether this is a true story, I do not know. But the story and the reigning impression of Tallulah Bankhead are a perfect fit. Tallulah was— her dates are 1902–1966—the beautiful Southern belle with entirely unedited, not to say foul-mouthed, speech added. She was the woman who said and did anything she wished. Her grandfather and uncle were U.S. senators from Alabama, her father was Speaker of the House. When she was forced into the hospital with a peritoneal infection, the result of boozing and partying and generally riotous living, upon her release, she called out to her physician, "Don't think that this has taught me a lesson." Tallulah Bankhead's was the charm of complete abandon—not in the least charming when practiced by men—the charm, as she might have put it, of simply not giving a fuck about anything.

To be in a position to do this, to live one's life so carelessly, certain prerequisites are necessary. For Tallulah they were dazzling youthful beauty, talent (in her case as a stage actress), and lots of money (earned on the stage). A girl who never knew her mother, who died a few weeks after giving birth to her, who was never her father's favorite daughter, who was a pudgy tomboy as a child, Tallulah nonetheless early sensed that hers would be a glittering life, and acted on that premonition. She threw tantrums, fits, and availed herself of other ploys that usually resulted in her getting her way.

Get her way Tallulah pretty much did through much of her life. At seventeen she secured a part in a Broadway play, and was straightaway a hit, someone much talked about in New York. In her early twenties she moved to London, where her stage performances brought her even greater *réclame*. She became a central figure in smart society on two continents; friends with English royalty and the American wealthy. She went out to Hollywood for the money, which given the extravagance with which she lived she required in ample amounts. She never made the same impress in the movies that she had done on stage, but then neither did Hollywood make much of an impression on her. Her two great stage roles were those of Regina Giddens in Lillian Hellman's *The Little Foxes* and Blanche DuBois in Tennessee Williams' *Streetcar Named Desire*. Tennessee Williams claimed he wrote the part of Blanche with Tallulah in mind. In 1939 she was on the cover of *Life*, of which there could be no grander publicity coup. In 1950 she was the mistress of ceremonies of *The Big Show*, a radio variety program that in its day had the highest ratings in the land.

In the end Tallulah was more a celebrity than a performing artist. She was celebrated as a character, though a caricature perhaps comes closer to it. She had, to begin with, her wonderful name, Tallulah, which sounds like nothing so much as an exotic tropical flower. Then there was her voice, husky, dusky, with a touch of Southern drawl to it, exploited by every comic impressionist of the day, recognized by the entire nation. The television critic John Crosby claimed Tallulah's voice had "more timbre than Yellowstone National Park." Grain and texture were given to her voice by the 150 cigarettes she is supposed to have smoked daily. She was also a serious drinker, and did drugs, cocaine or whatever else you happen to have around the place. ("Cocaine isn't habit forming, dahling," she said. "I should know. I've been using it for years.")

Tallulah's sex life was, to understate the matter a touch, gaudy. As a ballpark figure, she claimed to have slept with 5,000 men. She was heterosexual, she was homosexual, she was completely sexual. ("I've had a man and I've had a woman," she said, "and there's got to be something better.") An insomniac who couldn't bear to be alone, a logorrheic in need of a full-time audience, she used sex as a (generally ineffective) soporific.

Like Judy Garland, Tallulah had a large male following of gay men. They were known, *New Yorker* theater critic Brendan Gill reports, as her "caddies." The name derives from the fact that many among them ran errands for her; her life being in a permanent state of chaos, she had many errands to run. At her theatrical performances, Gill also reports, the caddies could be disruptive, caring chiefly for the campier bits in her acting, the bits when she was most Tallulah-esque.

Funny things Tallulah said tended to get around. During an intermission at a Maeterlinck play that she attended with the *New York Times* theater critic Alexander Woollcott, she said, "There's less here than meets the eye," a remark that Woollcott put in his review in the next day's paper, launching Tallulah as a wit. "What's the matter, dahling," she is supposed to have said when introduced to a man at a party, "don't you recognize me with my clothes on?" She minored in non sequiturs: "We've just been reminiscing about the future," she once said. Or, again: "I'd like to kiss you, dahling, but I've just washed my hair."

"I wish I had my life to live again. I'd make the same mistakes, only sooner," is a remark of Tallulah's that gives off a sad ping of autobiographical truth. Tallulah had two failed marriages, neither of which produced children. Instead of children she had lovers and, at one point, a lion cub that she kept as a house pet. She was a spendthrift, of everything, not just money but time, energy, people—she used them all up. Emotional spendthrifts usually operate, like financial ones, on deficits, which soon enough catch up with them.

Tallulah's caught up with her when she reached her fifties. Hard living didn't do much for her looks, which were once thought so captivating. Her health began to go; heavy smoking entrapped her in emphysema. She began to mock her own behavior. "My heart is as pure as the driven slush," she said, adding, "Say anything you like about me so long as it isn't boring." The problem was that, no longer beautiful or richly talented, she eventually did become a bit of a bore, predictable in her outrageousness, which meant that the outrageousness itself became a touch pitiful.

Charmers, men or women, risk becoming bores in old age. People grew tired of the aging Tallulah's loquaciousness. "I've just spent an hour talking to Tallulah for a few minutes," the actor Fred Keating said. Profane language is more arresting coming from the mouth of a young and beautiful woman than from that of an aging woman with heavy smears of lipstick across her mouth. By her sixties Tallulah was ugly, and knew it—photographs of her in her last years bear out her self-estimate, for they all seem as if the lens were blurred—ugly enough not to wish to be seen before a large public. She was at Truman Capote's famous party at the Plaza in 1966 where the guests wore masks, else she probably wouldn't have attended. Complications from emphysema drove her into St. Luke's Hospital in New York, where she made life hell for the staff, before sinking into a coma, and dying, at the age of sixty-six, with no one, including herself, wishing she had lived longer. Charm, too, can wear out its welcome; it's a mistake to stay too long at the party.

Audrey Hepburn's charm, almost diametrically different from Tallulah Bankhead's, never did wear out. Where Tallulah was aggressively loquacious, Audrey Hepburn came across as winningly reticent. Where Tallulah was shameless, Audrey Hepburn was, or certainly seemed, sensitive. Where Tallulah was unembarrassedly coarse, Audrey Hepburn was unfailingly refined. The two women serve to set the boundaries, north to south, of female charm.

Perhaps alone among movie stars, Audrey Hepburn was equally admired by women and men. Lots of women wished to look like her or yearned for her natural refinement or to be able to wear clothes as she did (with a helping hand here from Hubert de Givenchy); most men wished to protect her. She wasn't about sex, or at least sex wasn't the first thing one thought of when seeing her. She combined fragility and spriteliness, in a unique and immensely attractive way. Not for nothing did she regularly play in movies up against attractive older leading men: Gary Cooper, Gregory Peck, Henry Fonda, Humphrey Bogart, Cary Grant, William Holden, Fred Astaire, Rex Harrison. The attraction here was twofold: Their maturity meant they could protect her, and her youthfulness seemed to give them a second chance in life with a virginally fresh young woman.

In reality there was nothing especially virginal about Audrey Hepburn, who seems to have had normal sexual appetites and, for a movie star, a normally adventurous sexual life. She turns out to have had the best of taste in everything but men. She had a misfired engagement with a Canadian millionaire; a love affair with the alcoholic William Holden; another with the playwright Robert Anderson, who wrote a roman à clef about it; two bad marriages, producing a son each; and a twelve-year-long live-in relationship in Switzerland at the end of her life with a man who had formerly been Merle Oberon's much younger escort. If she had a weakness, it was in her choice of men; she was perhaps too passive, too ready to give herself over to men who wished to control her. Or was she instead one of those women E. M. Forster once described in *Howards End* as "stimulated by worthlessness in men." The leading offender in the worthlessness category may have been her first husband, Mel Ferrer, quite as wretched a husband as he was an actor.

No one has ever quite been able to nail Audrey Hepburn's physical quality. *Gamin, elfin, sprite, fey* are among the words most often hauled out to do so, but none quite fits. In his splendid biography of Audrey Hepburn, Donald Spoto quotes a woman named Aud Johanssen, who danced with the young Audrey Hepburn in the chorus on the London stage, saying: "I have the biggest tits onstage, but everyone looks at the girl who has none at all."

Audrey Hepburn was five foot seven inches and weighed 110 pounds with a twenty-inch waist. More than anything else she longed to be the ballet dancer she so much appeared by nature physically intended to be. History, however, ruled otherwise. Her late girlhood and early adolescence, the time of crucial training for a ballerina, were spent at her grandparents' home in Arnhem, in Holland, under the Nazi occupation. The same age as Anne Frank, whom she somewhat resembled, she lived under a reign of fear, ill-nourished—at one point the family diet was chiefly tulip bulbs— always expecting the worst. "I knew the cold clutch of human terror all through my teens," she later said. She was sixteen when the war was over, too late to make up the lost years of training to achieve her dream of becoming a prima ballerina.

She also suffered the loss of a father, a ne'er-do-well named Joseph Hepburn-Ruston, English on his father's side, French and Dutch on his mother's, who met and married Audrey's mother, a Dutch baroness, in what was then the Dutch colony of Indonesia. A fascist, he was a supporter in England of Oswald Moseley, and he and Audrey's mother actually lunched with Hitler before the war. Her father married her mother for her money, and left her and his young daughter when he had run through it. Audrey Hepburn grew up fatherless. This crushing fact weighed heavily on her lifelong insecurity and intermittent bouts of depression.

Some of these hardships in Audrey Hepburn's life worked to her advantage. She grew up, for example, tri-lingual, speaking English, Dutch, and French (her mother and father lived for a spell in Belgium), which gave her an odd but appealing accent. She had, in effect, no mother tongue. "There is no speech I can relax into when I'm tired," she said, "because my ear has never been accustomed to one intonation." Her speech, sounding mid-Atlantic with a slight hesitation to it, was like no one else's and part of the appealing signature of her performance.

Success came to her early. In 1953, when she was twenty-four, she won both an Oscar (for *Roman Holiday*) and a Tony (for *Ondine*) and many other awards beside. She never thought herself a first-class actress, but she had something quite as good as acting ability; she had natural charm. Audiences liked to look at her, listen to her, root for her. In her movies and in her life, she never lacked for a following.

Her good taste extended to her choice of movie roles, with only a few exceptions (*War and Peace, Green Mansions,* and *The Unforgiven* perhaps most notable among them). She seemed to know what was best for her particular talent. From *Roman Holiday* through *Nun's Story, Two for the*

Road, Funny Face, My Fair Lady to *Robin and Marian*—all seemed roles made for her. Her taste in directors—William Wyler, Bill Wilder, Fred Zinnemann, Stanley Donen, Blake Edwards, George Cukor—wasn't bad either.

Audrey Hepburn was chary of giving interviews. They made her nervous, doubtless because she recognized that there was something inherently wrong, cheapening even, in talking about oneself. When forced to give an interview to promote a film, she put off all questions about her personal life. Later in life she savvily turned down an interview request from Barbara Walters; savvily because to be asked about one's personal life by Barbara Walters is automatically to forfeit one's claim to charm by falling into the slough of vulgarity. No one ever would think to call Audrey Hepburn vulgar.

On the personal front, she had things to hide. The fragility that was part of her film persona was also part of her actual life. She was delicately wired, and at different points in her life—she had five miscarriages and gave birth to a stillborn child—suffered nervous breakdowns. She did all she could to keep her failed marriages out of the press. Although she was rich, famous, beautiful, "rarely," said her press agent Henry Rogers, "did I see her happy."

To hide one's depression, disguise one's defeats, show modesty in the face of enormous success, such are the ingredients for charm operating at a high level. In her quiet way, Audrey Hepburn was a great lady, and greatness, coming from unexpected quarters, is charming. About that charm there seems to be no disagreement, even among tough critics. Fred Zinnemann, who directed *The Nun's Story*, said of her: "I have never seen anyone more disciplined, more gracious or more dedicated to her work than Audrey. There was no ego, no asking for extra favors; there was the greatest consideration for her co-workers." Stanley Donen, who directed her in *Two for the Road* and *Funny Face*, said: "Her magnetism was so extraordinary that everyone wanted to be close to her. It was as if she placed a glass barrier between herself and the world. You couldn't get behind it easily. It made her remarkably attractive." Alfred Lunt said: "She has authentic charm. Most people simply have nice manners." And Billy Wilder, who didn't in the least mind knocking actors he directed, said:

"Audrey was known for something which has disappeared, and that is elegance, grace and manners . . . God kissed her on the cheek, and there she was."

Donald Spoto tells that Mel Ferrer and Audrey Hepburn's agent thought she ought to collect a royalty of some sort for allowing Hubert de Givenchy to use her name in connection with his successful perfume *L'Interdit*. Givenchy was even ready to do so, but Hepburn said absolutely not.

I don't want anything from Hubert. I don't need his money—he's my friend. If I've helped him build his perfume business, then that's exactly what one friend should do for another. If someone else offered me a million dollars to endorse a perfume, I would do it—but Hubert is my friend. I don't want anything. Yes, I even want to walk into a drugstore and buy the perfume at the retail price.

For the last five or so years of her life—she died at sixty-four—Audrey Hepburn worked seven or eight months of the year for UNICEF. She visited Somalia and Ethiopia, and did so without any of the perks expected by the high-level celebrity that she indubitably was: She flew coach, rode in trucks, ate the same food as everyone else. Always a nervous public speaker, she nonetheless gave endless speeches in the attempt to arouse interest in and raise money for the plight of starving children in Africa and Asia, and the speeches were apparently effective. A good heart on display, such as Audrey Hepburn possessed, one free of falsity and fakery, might itself be a strong definition of charm.

Tallulah Bankhead and Audrey Hepburn, as I noted, describe the wide boundaries of modern female charm. Much charm, of course, lies within those boundaries—and also much false charm. I, for one, never found Jacqueline Kennedy Onassis especially charming. She was supposed to stand for refinement, high culture, art. Yet it all seemed so staged, which is to say unnatural, false, and therefore unconvincing. Everything in this act blew apart when Jacqueline Kennedy became Jackie O. by marrying Aristotle Onassis, a coarse billionaire, making plain that refinement, high culture, art wasn't at all what she was about. What she was about, and had been all along, despite the heavy screen of public relations and image-making, was money. Jacqueline Kennedy was attempting to play Audrey Hepburn, outside the movies, until her love first for power and then for money, by becoming evident, ruined the act.

Lillian Hellman was well on her way to being considered among the most charming of American women. She was a party-goer and a party-giver. Anyone who mattered in American cultural life was at one time or another a guest at her home on Martha's Vineyard. Her plays and screen-writing had made her wealthy. Her long-standing love affair with Dashiell Hammett, a man hounded by the House UnAmerican Affairs Commit-tee, somehow added to her luster. Most impressive of all she had faced down that same House on UnAmerican Affairs Committee. When asked to name the names of people in Hollywood and on Broadway whom she knew to be members of the Communist party, she said: "I cannot cut my conscience to fit this year's pattern," a remark which went instantly into all the books of quotations and made her a heroine of liberal American culture. At the Oscar Awards one year she received a standing ovation. From that time on, cynical friends said, she would accept only standing ovations.

Everyone who knew her attested that Lillian Hellman was fun to be with. A friend of mine reported that once, when Arthur Schlesinger entered a restaurant with his much taller wife, Lillian wondered aloud to my friend "whether he went up on her." She was a member of the edi-torial board of a magazine I edited, and, though I never saw her in comic mode, she could be penetrating in her observations. She once told me that there were two Edmund Wilsons: the one for men was the intellectual equivalent of the playground bully, who had to best other men by showing that he knew more than they no matter what the subject; then there was the Edmund Wilson for women, who could be seductive, avuncular, sweet.

Lillian was never beautiful, though through her liveliness she attracted many lovers. When I met her she was in her late sixties, and had lost such feminine attractiveness as she might once have possessed. With her rigidly permanented white hair and bony face, she looked like nothing so much as a figure in one of those paintings of the men who had signed the Declaration of Independence. Still, one wanted her approval; as a younger man, I at least did. I recall feeling pleased when she complimented me on something I had written.

When Lillian Hellman began publishing her memoirs in 1969, reviewers lined up to praise her. Although it was before I met her, I, in *The New Republic,* was among them. I then wrote that her first volume of memoirs, *An Unfinished Woman,* was "the work of a woman at once knowing yet without cynicism, tough yet generous, honest yet reticent." I was wrong, as it turned out, on all counts. Further on in her publication of her memoirs, in the volume called *Pentimento,* she told a story about helping defeat the Nazis through smuggling $50,000 to an anti-Nazi spy whom she calls Julia. The story was made into a movie, with Jane Fonda playing the Lillian Hellman part. Later the woman who was in fact the anti-Nazi spy wrote a book in which she made it clear that Lillian Hellman had done nothing of the kind she described in her memoir. She had made it up; she, who stood for truth unvarnished, was a bit of a fraud. The bad press she derived from this was redoubled when she sued the writer Mary McCarthy for calling her a liar; McCarthy said that "every word she writes is a lie, including 'and' and 'the.'" Hellman sued, not a thing one writer is supposed to do to another, especially a writer of liberal reputation, and the stock of her reputation fell even further.

Lillian had always been very political, but in her last years her politics tended to push aside her charm entirely. Too many of her sentences were festooned with the paranoid initials CIA and FBI. I recall walking with her one day to a restaurant in Washington, DC, after an editorial board meeting of the magazine mentioned earlier. Another member, Paul Freund, the legal scholar, a learned and quietly subtle man, joined us. When Lillian asked Paul what his plans were for the summer, he said that he was going to spend part of it at the Strasbourg Institute. "Oh," said Lillian, "is that still run by the CIA?" Without losing a step or breaking a smile, Paul Freund said, "I don't think so, Lillian. The food's not very good."

My last, still vivid picture of Lillian Hellman occurred that evening, sitting at the end of a large table in a French restaurant, picking at her food, a lit cigarette in hand, in an alcoholic haze, lonely in a crowd, another sad case of young charmers devolving into old bores.

Many women have of course been charming, but unless they wrote or were filmed or appear in other people's memoirs, we cannot know about the nature and extent of their charm. Everyone spoke kindly about Mrs. Isabella Stewart Gardner (1840–1924), the founder of the Boston Museum named after her; George Santayana claimed she was the only person he ever met who never gossiped. But how charming, precisely, she was cannot be known.

My friend, writer Midge Decter, has always seemed to me to qualify as charming. Midge is one of those women who one feels can see through any sham, not least one's own, which tends to put one, in her company, on one's best intellectual behavior. Her specialty is in saying the important obvious thing when everyone else seems to have forgotten it. In the early days of the second wave of feminism, when feminists argued that they were tired of women being treated as "sexual objects," Midge remarked to me, "Sexual objects, hell, I never slept with any man I didn't wish to sleep with." On another occasion, at a conference about the family, I watched her get up to say that her own family of late had given her much to worry about. Her elderly parents and in-laws were not well settled and had lots of medical problems; she had various disagreements with her children; she wasn't altogether pleased with the way some of her grandchildren were being raised. "No," she said, "the family is fraught with every kind of complication and worry, and I've just about had it with the family. But when I see who is attacking the family, I am determined to defend the damn thing." A perfect Midge Decter performance.

Other women have had reputations for wit. Wit can add to charm but in itself is not necessarily charming. No one was wittier than Oscar Wilde, yet Noël Coward called him "a tiresome affected sod," adding, "what a silly, conceited, inadequate creature he was and what a dreadful self-deceiver. It is odd that such brilliant wit should be allied to no humour at all." Dorothy Parker was witty, perhaps the wittiest American woman of the past century. Much of her wit, though, was cruel, in the nature of put-downs. She was also a serious boozer, and it is impossible to be drunk and charming, at least seriously drunk, which a good part of the time Parker was.

A successful Hollywood agent named Sue Mengers was notable for saying amusing things. She once entered a large party in Los Angeles and categorized the crowd there as "Schindler's B-List." She claimed her greatest achievement was not having any children. But, as Gertrude Stein once told Hemingway that "remarks are not literature," neither are remarks charm. Something different, something deeper is entailed.

The last, and most recent, candidate for charming woman in our day is Nora Ephron, the screenwriter, director, and essayist. In her movies—*When Harry Met Sally*, which she wrote, and *Sleepless in* Seattle, *You've Got Mail*, and *Julie and Julia*, which she wrote and directed, Nora Ephron attempted to revive, by bringing up-to-date, the great romantic comedies of an earlier era, comedies whose staple was charm. She was herself immensely attracted to charm, charming people, charming food and furniture and clothes, the charming life.

For those who didn't know her, Nora Ephron has left a record of her personality in her essays, which are almost entirely autobiographical. Her breakthrough essay "A Few Words about Breasts" (1972), appearing in *Esquire,* set the tone for the kind of writing that, after working five years as a reporter for the *New York Post*, brought her renown. The point of this essay is that Nora Ephron had small breasts as a girl and young woman, and it bothered her terribly. In tonally perfect anecdotes—about buying bras, petting with boys in high school, worrying about being found sexually inadequate for a husband—she makes plain, with comic touches added, how troubling not having large breasts was, especially in the 1950s when she came of age, the time of the amply bosomed Jane Russell, Jayne Mansfield, Marilyn Monroe, Sophia Loren, Elizabeth Taylor. The penultimate paragraph of her essay takes up the inconvenience of having large breasts about which women who have them sometimes complain. The final paragraph reads: "I have thought about their remarks, tried to put myself in their place, considered their point of view. I think they are full of shit."

Candor was at the center of Nora Ephron's charm. She attempted to undercut standard morality and conventional wisdom, received opinions by a strong dose of confessional truth. Or, if her own actions turned out to be conventional, such as dying her hair to ward off the appearance of aging, or being addicted to e-mail, or being naturally greedy at the prospect of an inheritance, she found clever ways of undercutting her own conventionality by highlighting it through comic self-deprecation. "Everything is copy," her mother once told her, and Nora Ephron seems to have lived her life with that as a motto.

Nora Ephron came of age as a writer in the early 1970s. *Esquire*, in which she had a column and was the magazine's only notable woman writer, was the hot magazine of the day. Although brought up in Los Angeles, where both her parents wrote for the movies, she became a New Yorker, the most fervent kind of New Yorker, not the born but the naturalized version. She lived for a time in Washington, DC, when she was married to her second husband (of three) Carl Bernstein, the investigative reporter who, with Bob Woodward, helped unveil the Watergate scandal. When she discovered that Bernstein was cheating on her with the wife of the then English ambassador, she divorced him and afterward wrote a novel about it called *Heartburn*, later made into a movie with Meryl Streep as Nora and Jack Nicholson as Carl Bernstein. "Everything," like her mother said, "is copy."

Beginning in the 1960s, a woman named Erma Bombeck wrote a popular column, mostly run in small-town newspapers, about the trials of being a woman, mother, and wife in suburban America. She would not have liked to hear it, but Nora Ephron became an Erma Bombeck for the hip upper-middle class, with talent added. These would be the people who live in Manhattan and Los Angeles and San Francisco, perhaps in Portland and Seattle. They care enormously about food. Many of them at one time or another were probably in psychotherapy. A good address means a lot to them. So, too, do clothes and hairdos. They are nervous about child-rearing, about sex, especially about seeming in any way out of it.

Erma Bombeck was cute, Nora Ephron clever, but in the end it came to pretty much the same thing: Both women mocked that which they were going to continue doing anyhow. The note of self-deprecation is the reigning one in much of Nora Ephron's writing. "Sometimes I think not having to worry about your hair is the upside of death," she wrote. "So, twice a week, I go to a beauty salon and have my hair blown dry. It's cheaper by far than psychoanalysis, and much more uplifting." Once in one of these beauty shops she "picked up a copy of *Vogue* while having my hair done, and it cost me twenty thousand dollars. But you should see my teeth."

She mentions the admirable manner in which a male friend died, but before dying arranging to send back love letters sent to him by women in his youth. She then notes that if she were to do the same, the men would be mystified. "I haven't heard from any of these men for years, and on the evidence, they all seem to have done an extremely good job of getting over me." Sometimes, though, the comedy lapses into the sadness of the rich, with-it life, and she touches on its truth. She writes about the deep pleasure in being in her (second) Long Island home on the Fourth of July with her third and final husband, Nick Pileggi, and their children. "There were fireworks at the beach, and we would pack a picnic, dig a hole in the sand, build a fire, sing songs—in short, experience a night when we felt like a conventional American family (instead of the divorced patched-together, psychoanalyzed, oh-so-modern family we were)."

Nora Ephron was not beautiful—with her $20,000 teeth and the rest of her expensive grooming, she looked instead New York upper-east East Side high-maintenance—but she was talented. She wrote and directed movies, no easy task, and they are movies that people greatly enjoyed. Her essays were best-seller pleasing, though rarely touched the profound (as in the quotation above about life on Long Island on the Fourth of July). She left an estate estimated at $15 million. When she died, in 2012, in her seventy-first year, the feeling of loss among people who knew her, professionally and personally, seemed entirely genuine. She would have adored being thought charming, for in her movies and her writing attempting to charm is what she set out to do. In the contemporary world, though, it may not be easy for a woman to be charming. So many things have changed that now stand in the way.

When Audrey Hepburn retired from making movies she did so because she sensed that roles for women of the kind she did best—roles emphasizing refinement, elegance, delicate beauty—were no longer available, or perhaps even believable. Something had happened, to the society, to the culture, that made the distance required for female charm to make itself felt no longer quite possible. A strong component of female charm was the reticence and careful distancing that allowed for mystery, specifically female mystery. In our day, reticence has been replaced by candor, distancing by unwanted intimacy, and the loser has been that element of mystery that has always been absolutely essential to womanly charm.

CHAPTER IX

Vulgar Charmers

ONE TENDS TO THINK OF THE CHARMING AS SUAVE, URBANE, REFINED, ELE-
gant, worthy not only of admiration but, the perhaps far-fetched hope is,
of emulation. Not all charmers fit this description. Some approximate near
the reverse, and yet are still charming, though not of course to everyone.
Such is the multifacetedness of charm that a small number of people who
could not care less about being charming, set out even to be the reverse
of charming, nevertheless turn out to be so.

These are the vulgar charmers. What makes them vulgar is their lack
of interest in good taste. Taste itself, the very idea of it, would seem not
to exist for them. I write "would seem," but of course it just doesn't, flat-
out. Good taste exists for them only to travesty, to violate, to outrage. If
traditionally charming people can be counted upon to exhibit good taste,
the vulgar charmers can equally be counted on to mock and execrate it.

Good taste, after all, is a construct, and far from a permanent one.
Anyone who thinks it is permanent should be reminded that at Versailles,
at the court of Louis XIV, the great Sun King defecated behind a screen
with his courtiers standing about, certain among them designated to hold
his bowl, others to clean him up afterward. Acceptable good taste, in
other words, can change radically, has its limits, and is sometimes worth
debunking if done in an amusing way. Making bad taste amusing is one of
the things the vulgar charmers do. The pleasure they provide derives from
watching standard good conduct ignored, decorum trashed. Not, this, to
be sure, everybody's idea of a good time, but for many of us somehow
charming nonetheless.

The first vulgar charmer, a character not from real life but from literature, is Falstaff, fat, sensual, a drinking man, bawdy, a small-time swindler, cowardly, witty, and withal winning. So irresistible is he that Shakespeare used him in three different plays, and Verdi brought him front and center from supporting actor to be the main and eponymous subject of his opera *Falstaff*. In Shakespeare, when Prince Hal ascends to be king, it is understood he must reject Falstaff, putting him aside, as *Corinthians* instructs when we grow older we ought to put aside childish things, but not without regrets. No one in real life would want to be Falstaff, but so long as he is on stage, neither, such is his charm, does anyone wish him to leave.

Returning from literature and from the seventeenth century to today, consider the comedian and movie director Mel Brooks, whose immensely successful career has been built on cleverly exhibiting bad taste. Brooks has made comic movies joking about the Nazis (*The Producers*), hunchbacks (*Young Frankenstein*), flatulent and racists cowboys (*Blazing Saddles*), bird-droppings *(High Anxiety)*, and gay men in Sherwood Forest (*Men in Tights*). He has operated as if etiquette were of no concern, political correctness did not exist, good taste laughable—and got away with it. He makes wretched jokes such as the one about the peacoat that would never have caught on if the man who invented it hadn't changed its original name from that of the urine coat. And people adore him for such stuff.

Interviewed on *60 Minutes* by the abrasive Mike Wallace, whom no one ever accused of being charming, Mel Brooks, instead of answering Wallace's opening question, asked him instead where he got his watch and how much he paid for it. In response to Wallace's second question, Brooks leaned over, rubbed Wallace's lapel, and exclaimed upon what a fine fabric it was, and asked what he paid for a jacket like that. What Brooks was doing, of course, was his interpretation of the crass Jew. The result was to crack up Wallace, born Myron Leon Wallik and himself Jewish. Brooks, Brooklyn-born, was originally Melvin Kaminsky.

Always brandishing his Jewishness, with a face more Jewish than a dill pickle, Mel Brooks ought to be embarrassing, especially to the Jews. But, somehow, he isn't. He is also someone who doesn't seem to mind bringing up bodily functions—belching and below—that no conventionally charming person would ever do. This, too, in his goofy presentation doesn't seem to offend. A standard Mel Brooks anecdotal joke is the one he tells about informing his traditionally Jewish mother that he was going to marry the actress Anne Bancroft, a Catholic, and her response being, "That's fine. I'll be in the kitchen; my head'll be in the oven."

Deliberately coarse and crude, Brooks was never salacious. In his movies he left this to the comedienne Madeline Kahn, who was able to take the heat out of sexuality through comedy. He also has an odd courtliness. He is raucous but never mean. One senses no put-down, no one-upmanship, no malice in him. He can be wild, but he is not vicious nor in the least dangerous. However rocky the comedic flight he takes his audiences out on, they may be fairly certain that he will bring them back and will land the plane safely.

The comic actor Gene Wilder, who was featured in *The Producers* and in *Blazing Saddles,* said that Mel Brooks told him "never to be afraid of offending. It's when you worry about offending people that you get in trouble." Both in his movies and in his interviews—and no one gives more charming interviews than he—Brooks is always gambling. What he says and has done on screen can cause people either to cringe or to roar with laughter—falling off the couch laughter, dangerous laughter, the kind with the threat of heart attack in it. Wilder said of his friend Brooks: "Sometimes he's vulgar and unbalanced, but . . . I know that little maniac is a genius. A loud kind of Jewish genius—maybe that's as close as you can get to defining him. As for his vulgarity, which cannot be argued away, it is indubitably a healthy vulgarity."

And so has been that of many of the greatest modern comedians. The Marx Brothers' movies, taken together, were a concerted attack on what passes for good taste. They were put on to this when at Metro-Goldwyn-Mayer the producer Irving Thalberg, impressed by their comic energy, felt that they wanted a target for their anarchic humor. "Throwing a snowball at a man isn't funny," he instructed them, "but throwing a snowball and knocking off his silk top hat is funny." Thalberg's notion was that the Marx Brothers would be a lot funnier if they played their comedy against rigid social institutions; and so they did, making charmingly vulgar movies against the background of opera, higher education, psychiatry and the medical profession generally, first-class ocean travel, thoroughbred racing, and high society. The best part of the Marx Brothers' career was devoted to knocking off silk top hats.

The release from good taste is the message behind the better Marx Brothers' movies. "The reason people enjoy to see us doing any damn fool thing that comes into our head is quite simple," said Chico Marx. "It's because that's how a normal person would like to act, once in a while." Havoc was the Marx Brothers' specialty, their underlying collective message that respectable life was a sham, a scam, a swindle. And yet their movies are now regarded as classic, the Marx Brothers themselves as loveable.

Even profanity, properly deployed, can be charming. I have long admired W. C. Fields' work in this line, where it comes out not in his movies but in the anecdotes that have come down about him. Apparently a young man was going about Hollywood claiming to be Fields' illegitimate son, a claim Fields utterly rejected. One day the young man showed up at Fields' home, there to be greeted by the butler. When the butler asked Fields how he should deal with this young man, Fields replied, in his famous slow drawl, "Tell him something equivocal, like go fuck yourself." The charm, if not the genius, is of course in the formulation: the word equivocal paired with perhaps the least equivocal command in the English language.

Zero Mostel, on the other hand, can be terribly amusing but not at all charming. Mostel was the man who first snapped his fingers to accompany his singing of "If I Were a Rich Man," and then added *deedle deedle deedle dee* to the chorus of the song. Many anecdotes have been told about his wild spontaneity. One has a friend tell him that he has a touch of butter on his sleeve, which causes Mostel to grab the butter dish and proceed to butter his arm all the way up the shoulder. Amusing, as I say, but far from charming.

The difference between being amusing and being charming is that charm is more universal in its appeal. I, for example, have found the comedian Don Rickles intermittently amusing. ("Frank Sinatra saved my life. One night in a parking lot in Vegas. He said, 'That's enough, boys.'") Mae West is perhaps the first well-known vulgar female charmer. ("Is that a comb in your pocket," she is supposed to have told a man playing opposite her, "or are you just glad to see me?") On occasion I have found Joan Rivers amusing ("I don't see why everyone is so down on Prince Charles and Camilla. I was honored that they invited me to their wedding. I couldn't go, but I did send a gift: a George Foreman Grill."), but never charming. Sarah Silverman's faux naïve Jewish princess bits attacking political correctness is giggle-making (After describing all the inopportune times for her to have had a child, she says, "I guess the best time to have a child is when you are a black teenager."), but again well short of charming. Amusing makes one smile, chortle, laugh; charming sometimes does all this, too, but is also, somehow, endearing.

Jackie Gleason was amusing and charming both. He was charming in many roles, as the sadly bumptious bus driver Ralph Kramden; as Reginald von Gleason III, the ridiculously inept playboy; the talkative Joe the Bartender; the Poor Soul; and just about any other character he cared to play. He was perhaps at his most charming in *The Hustler*, where he played the pool shark Minnesota Fats, to which he brought a suavity and delicacy that only an overweight man in perfect command of his body could achieve. Jackie Gleason was also charming as himself, the overweight, heavy-drinking, extravagant show business figure. No one would wish to be Jackie Gleason, no one could be Jackie Gleason, but to be in his company might, at least for brief spells, be charming.

Louie Prima makes the cut as a vulgar charmer. How easily he is imagined slurping up a huge dish of pasta in a wife-beater undershirt at a kitchen table on Staten Island, even though he was born in New Orleans and may never have seen a kitchen table after the age of thirty. When his wife, the stone-faced Keeley Smith, sang "I Got It Bad and That Ain't Good," there behind her Louie was, with the refrain, "I Got It Good, and That Ain't Bad," his eyes rolled back, his tongue lolling out of his mouth. He came across as lower-class Italian, heavy accent on the *I*, the white musician's Louis Armstrong, but with deliberate coarseness added. Refinement was no part of his being. Not everyone found this charming. I'm not sure that women found Prima as amusing as did men. Louie Prima's charm was a specialized taste, like that for heavily garlicked Italian dishes.

The comedian Larry David is another specialist in trashing good taste. His specialty is to go right up to the line of bad taste—and then cross it. Most of the plots on *The Larry David Show* are propelled by his lapses in good taste. On one of his shows he claimed a cough owing to oral sex; he will use the one word—the c-word—not permitted even in the most permissive social circles; he has made the earnest argument that men do better to urinate sitting down; he has claimed a dog bit him on his penis; he brought a black comedian on his show doing ghetto humor that causes every progressive to shudder. Funny, some of it, chiefly because no one would have thought a comedian would have gone quite so far, even in the open purlieus of cable television. Larry David has built his career on such stuff. He is a funny man but not one anyone would ever think to call charming.

Working the same rich field of undermining good taste yet coming away charming was Sid Caesar, who in the 1950s was the premier comedian on American television. A large man, slightly gross in mien, with a face of great plasticity, a stutterer (though not when doing his comedy), said to have had a drinking problem, Caesar was able to provoke Mel Brooks' dangerous laughter, and to do so with regularity. This was perhaps partly owing to Brooks being one of his battery of splendid comedy writers: Also among them were Neil Simon, Larry Gelbart, Woody Allen, Selma Diamond, Mel Tolkin, Carl Reiner, and Howie Morris—an all-star team, a murderer's row, of comic writers. But it was in greater part owing to Sid Caesar himself, who understood how vulgar charm worked, that his show was the immense success it was.

Sid Caesar did not do jokes but sketch comedy. Sketch comedy took on the little oddities of people, or the strange situations in which they find themselves, and wrung laughter from them. The couple at the opera finding themselves seated too close to the percussion section. An unsophisticated couple not knowing how much to tip a headwaiter to get a decent table. The effect on yet another married couple of a beautiful single woman moving into the apartment next door. Sketch comedy drew from the quotidian. "We had the ability to extract humor out of everyday life," Caesar wrote in his autobiography.

Sid Caesar was a Jewish *schtarker*, or strong man, and was able to give these playlets a physical turn. (His two brothers, Abe and Dave, were, respectively, six feet four inches and six feet, two inches; he was himself six one.) In a sketch called "My Life Story," a parody of a once hugely popular television show called *This Is Your Life*, Caesar, playing the man whose life it is, is confronted by Howie Morris playing his Uncle Goopy, who, upon embracing Caesar after a long absence, refused to disengage, causing Caesar to carry him, pending from his neck, through the better part of the sketch. In another sketch, Caesar is bitten by a termite who has just returned from a NASA mission in outer space, which gives him a termite-like appetite for wood, and he proceeds to eat his way through furniture and just about everything else wooden on the set. In another parody, this time of an Orson Welles movie called *The Stranger*, Caesar, Imogene Coca, Howie Morris, and Carl Reiner play clock tower figures who have run amok, beating one another up with hammers, anvils, and throwing water in one another's faces. What Caesar's television shows—first *The Show of Shows*, then *Caesar's Hour*—brought to television was a combination of wild invention and artful slapstick, of which Sid Caesar was a master.

Something earthy, old shoe, the reverse of elegant inhered in all that Sid Caesar did on television. His comedy shattered the notion that one could expect to live an easy and well-ordered life. This, in good part, is what gave him his charm. So many of the sketches he and his writers devised were attacks on pretense. This was his plan. In his autobiography, he tells that he began *Caesar's Hour* with a domestic sketch. "The truth never changes," he writes. "You still have to eat. You still fight with your wife. So starting each show with a domestic sketch was like shaking the audience's hands, making them feel at home."

As for his own part in all this, Caesar notes: "I set myself up as the clown, the fall guy, and the butt of the jokes. I was the self-assured guy who beneath it all was very insecure and kept screwing up. I was everybody's brother, cousin, and uncle. In every downtrodden situation and every fight with my wife, even the smallest triumph got laughs and sympathy from the audience . . . We also didn't preach. It was more important to get the laugh than to send the message."

Week after week, for roughly six years, beginning in 1950, Sid Caesar performed live on television, supplying humor that was topical yet somehow also timeless, wild yet never offensive, sometimes verging on the crude yet neither gross nor coarse. The humor also had an appeal across generations. *The Show of Shows* and later *Caesar's Hour* was television that three generations of the same family could watch together and all enjoy. To this day, sixty years later, people remember many of the extraordinary sketches on those shows.

The achievement was impressive, but it took its toll on Sid Caesar, a self-described obsessive compulsive who couldn't sleep nights wondering how he could have improved shows already done and worrying about those forthcoming. He took pills, overate, boozed heavily. One night in 1977, playing in Regina, Saskatchewan, in Canada, in Neil Simon's *The Last of the Red Hot Lovers,* he blanked out on his lines and realized that his drinking was destroying his mental capacities. He began psychotherapy, took a cold-turkey alcohol cure, dieted, and came out of it stripped of his neuroses, his alcoholism kicked, slender, and optimistic, but, as his account of this recovery in his autobiography fails to reveal, no longer amusing and rather boring in a self-congratulatory way. His career poses the artistic dilemma, not to be sure faced by all artists, of whether it is better to live with one's talent including all its wretched side effects or to live without these side effects and be stripped of one's talent. For some people, Sid Caesar among them, having it both ways evidently wasn't an option.

Dean Martin, another vulgar charmer, seems to have had no split whatsoever between his stage and personal life. Billy Wilder called Martin "the funniest man in Hollywood." What was the joke? For those who missed it, it was that Dean Martin simply didn't care—nothing, nada, zilch, he didn't give a rat's rump about anything. Which was the source of his charm, odd as that may at first sound.

Martin was born Dino Crocetti to immigrant parents in 1917 in Steubenville, Ohio. The town of Steubenville was what was then known as "wide-open." Prostitution, gambling, every sort of illicit pleasure was on the menu. Jimmy the Greek, the Vegas odds setter, came from Steubenville. The town resembled nothing so much as a minor league mafia franchise. Dino grew up with a sense of a more than merely imperfect but a deeply, permanently corrupted world.

Bored by school, which he left in the tenth grade, he was a genial screw off, with an early and as yet undeveloped talent for singing. He ran errands for the local gamblers, and at sixteen himself became a dealer in one of Steubenville's backroom casinos. He was tall, striking-looking, though shy of being smashingly handsome by having too large a nose. A local hustler pushed him into boxing, but he quickly decided there were easier ways to earn a living.

Singing was the less punishing career, and he began to sing in clubs in Steubenville and in nearby towns. One of the many agents he would acquire along the way had him change him name to Dino Martini; another, completing his de-Italianization, suggested he change it again, this time to Dean Martin. Bing Crosby was the great singer of the day, and the young Dean Martin, as did many other beginning crooners, modeled his voice and style on Crosby's.

A nonchalance, a coolness, a certain distant quality was part of Dean Martin's personality. (Joe DiMaggio also had this quality, minus the comedy and the singing talent.) This didn't come across so much cold as unavailable for intimacy. Rather than seek out other people, people tended to seek him out. As a singer, women were attracted by his good looks—fairly early in his career he had rhinoplasty, settling the nose problem—but men found that the songs he sang spoke to them. A winning combination of the manly and stylish and amusing came through in all he did.

When he sang about the moon hitting your eye like a big pizza pie, that's amore, something about him supplied a subtext that read, "Can you believe people pay me to sing such crap?" When he sang about going to Houston, you'd have to be a serious ninny not to realize that a man like him wouldn't spend twenty minutes in a town like Houston unless the fee paid him to do so was immense. "Goin' to Houston—whaddya, fuckin' kiddin' me?" his rendition of the song all but said. Late in his career, after his serious drinking had set in, one night in Las Vegas, before a large audience, he said, "I hate guys who sing songs serious."

Martin was on the slow rise as a nightclub singer, but he hit his stride when he joined with Jerry Lewis (born Joseph Levitch), a goofball comedian four years younger than he, then doing a record-miming act. One of the mysteries of show business is why certain comedy-couple acts work: Laurel and Hardy, Burns and Allen, Abbott and Costello, Olsen and Johnson. Dean Martin and Jerry Lewis were another such comedy-couple act.

Nick Tosches, Dean Martin's penetrating biographer, claims that their act was "a celebration of ignorance, absurdity, and stupidity," and so it seems when viewed today, when it no longer seems in the least funny.

Jerry Lewis admired what most men admired in Martin: his self-assurance and ability to view the world as essentially a joke, and a slightly off-colored one at that. Worry was for other people. Nick Tosches writes: "His uncaring air of romance reflected the flash and breezy sweet seductions of a world in which everything came down to broads, booze, and money, with plenty of linguine on the side."

The team of Martin and Lewis was booked into all the flashy nightclubs of the day—the Copacabana in New York, the Chez Paree in Chicago, Ciro's in Los Angeles—and at top prices. Their movies grossed tremendous sums; they had their own radio show; they were an international attraction. They did the first big charity telethon, for Muscular Dystrophy. (The comedian Lenny Bruce remarked that Jerry Lewis damn well ought to do something for muscular dystrophy, for with his various grimaces and spastic movements he may have caused a lot of it.) Between the middle 1940s and the middle 1950s, no act in show business was bigger than Martin and Lewis.

Through it all Dean Martin remained unfazed. Meeting the Queen of England did nothing for him. Later he would declare he thought John F. Kennedy a jerk and his brother Bobby a scumbag. Although invited, he didn't bother to go to the Kennedy inaugural. Nor did he have an especially good opinion of Frank Sinatra, who cultivated his friendship much more than Martin did Sinatra's. Martin thought Sinatra, with his hopeless love affairs and dopey marriages, always sucking up to Mafia guys and then the Kennedys and later the Reagans, rather pathetic. Dean Martin called everyone "pallie," the way Louis Armstrong called people "pops," but the fact was that he neither had nor wanted any close friends.

Not even his own success impressed Martin all that much. He was ready to throw it all away when he had had enough of Jerry Lewis, whom there is no strong evidence to suggest that he had ever much liked. When Lewis began to upstage him in their movies, he showed his irritation. Lewis' neediness and insecurity disgusted him. In desperation, Lewis claimed that it was their love for each other that made their act the extraordinary success it was. "You can talk about love all you want," Tosches reports Martin replying. "To me you're nothing but a dollar sign."

Jerry Lewis was a dollar sign Dean Martin was ready to walk away from, which he did, never to return, in 1956. The result was that Dean Martin, working alone, became even bigger. He became a star of stage, movies, and television, and his records did extremely well. In the 1960s he had an income of $15 million a year, not to mention vast real estate holdings. He was the enemy of phony showbiz sincerity, the malarkey of politicians, the falsity of romantic love. Nick Tosches describes the immense rating success of *The Dean Martin Show* by noting that "his uncaring manner and good-natured boorishness endeared him to the millions who were sick of sincerity, relevance, and pseudo-sophistication."

"Everybody loves somebody sometimes," Dean Martin sang, in a way that implied they do at least till somebody better comes along. "Everybody loves somebody," he ended his television show, "and remember I love all of you," neglecting to add, though it was implied, that if you believe that there is some real estate in the Everglades he'd like to show you.

Dean Martin's charm resided in good part in his detachment. He was thought to be a member in good standing in what was known as the Clan or the Rat Pack. In fact, he was contemptuous of Sammy Davis Jr., Peter Lawford, Joey Bishop, and the rest of them. He was good to his parents. He had three marriages and fathered seven children, but his second wife, Jeannie, the wife of longest duration, said that he wasn't someone who revealed his thoughts to anyone. His son, Dean Jr., said that he didn't really know his father very well. Apparently nobody did.

One of Martin's standby schticks was playing the amiable drunk. On a talk show he once said that he woke that very morning with so bad a hangover that his hair hurt. Before long his playing at being a drunk became a reality. He was also addicted to the painkiller Percodan, which he washed down with Scotch. As the national psyche became infused with political correctness, which he never for a moment recognized as worthy of his attention, he began to be reviled, at least in the press, for his tastelessness. He did a telethon for the City of Hope, causing the columnist Dorothy Kilgallen to ask, "Is leukemia an excuse for vulgarity?" Once admired for his casualness, the *Los Angeles Times* called him "the world's laziest superstar," and *Variety* added that he worked "in living ennui, [presenting] a better caricature of himself than any other impressionist." The old jokes about drinking and female anatomy and homosexuals no longer rang the gong of audience approval, and Dean Martin began to be chalked off as "tasteless." The finishing touch was when, in 1973, he married a woman thirty years younger than he. All these elements served to reduce what was once charming vulgarity to simple vulgarity, *tout court*. Dean Martin ended his life golfing, watching Westerns on television, getting slowly plastered daily, and awaiting death, which arrived in 1995—"Hiya, pallie"—when he was seventy-eight.

Charm, like cashmere, can wear thin.

CHAPTER X

Gay Charmers

CHARM, AS I HOPE I HAVE ESTABLISHED, COMES IN MANY VARIETIES: THERE ARE English, French, and Italian charmers; rogue charmers; female charmers; vulgar charmers; and doubtless many others, including, I would say, gay charmers. By this I do not mean merely gay men and lesbian women who also happen to be charming. What I mean is there is something about being gay or lesbian that, properly deployed, can confer a certain point of view and manner of confronting the world that is, or at least often can be in imaginative people, distinct and discretely different from other varieties of charm—a category of charm informed by a point of view conferred by the experience of being gay.

Somerset Maugham, who was himself gay, in an essay on El Greco in *Don Fernando*, his book on Spain, wrote of the gay man: "He stands on the bank, aloof and ironical, and watches the river of life flow on." This is of course less so today, when the acceptance of homosexuality is greatly increased, so that gay men and lesbian women now marry and raise families, and are often enough fully and rightly in the flow of life. Yet there is still, I believe, a homosexual outlook that provides its own kind of charm.

Until fairly recently, then, when strong prejudice against homosexuality was regnant, the gay man or lesbian woman was simultaneously inside and yet not completely of society. In many countries, and in several American states, homosexuality was illegal, an offense punished by imprisonment. This lent an outsider status to gay men, less so to lesbian women. In sophisticated circles, usually artistic ones, homosexuality generally caused no social difficulties, and the roster of homosexual artists has always been impressive. In the past century it has included such figures as Gertrude Stein, Jean Cocteau, E. M. Forster, Andre Gide, Somerset Maugham, Genet, Christopher Isherwood, W. H. Auden, Gore Vidal, James Baldwin, and many others. The earlier roster of homosexual artists, stretching from Michelangelo to Marcel Proust, is more impressive still. Even within artistic circles people could use another person's homosexuality against him or her in cruel ways—consider Ernest Hemingway's treatment of Gertrude Stein's lesbianism in *A Moveable Feast*—but among artists at least for the most part homosexuality found acceptance. Elsewhere things were trickier, and sometimes perilous. As recently as 1953, the great English actor John Gielgud was arrested for "importuning for immoral purposes"—in plainer language, for propositioning a man in a public restroom—and luckily escaped prison.

This sense of outsiderishness, tinged with genuine danger, gave gay and lesbian women imbued with wit a certain edge. If one were homosexual, one was like everyone else, but with a not insignificant difference—a difference still not adequately defined by scientific inquiry. Much talk and writing exists about the links—genetic, psychological, social-scientific—between homosexuality and artistic creativity, none of it scientifically confirmed. But what seems unarguable is that homosexuality has consequences on the ways in which one views the world—warily, sometimes skeptically, or, as Maugham suggests, detached and ironically. Because of this, gay men and lesbian women were endowed with a sensibility of a kind unavailable to others. This sensibility often issues in what I think of as gay charm.

Such charm, as with heterosexual charm, comes in various modes and styles. One thinks of Fran Lebowitz, who makes no bones about her lesbianism and who has said many charming and also a few penetrating things. On noting so many older children still being pushed in strollers, she remarked, "The person will make a fortune who invents the first shaving mirror for strollers." She has said that the reason for the paucity of her own writing is that she suffers from no mere writer's block but from a writer's blockade. She declared that she thought of her lesbianism as a badge of freedom—from the constraints, one gathers, of raising a family and participating in all the boring rituals that follow therefrom—and claimed now to be astonished to discover that the gay liberation movement is eager to have its adherents enrolled in two of the most constraining institutions in the land: marriage and the right to serve in the military.

In the view of some, Gore Vidal was thought to have been charming. Vidal could be witty, but his wasn't an amused but an angry wit. The form it chiefly took was the put-down. He is probably more famous for his dustups with William F. Buckley Jr., Norman Mailer, and Truman Capote than for anything he wrote. Vidal's was the pose of the patrician, based, rather flimsily, on having an ancestor who was a senator from Tennessee. His persistent attacks on the United States suggested that the country had somehow let him down, wasn't good enough for him. So, too, had contemporary literature, both in its creation and its criticism, though when he said disparaging things about either, one sensed that behind this was the failure of the literary establishment to recognize him as a great novelist, which, inconveniently enough, he wasn't. "I never pass up a chance to have sex or appear on television," was one of his better-known mots. Another has it that "It is not enough to succeed. Others must fail," which reads like La Rochefoucauld without the elegance.

Vidal was not amused by life, and, one felt, ticked off by not being allowed all the way inside, perhaps as a U.S. senator himself. (In 1960 he ran for Congress from New York's 29th congressional district and lost.) During his lawsuit against Truman Capote for slander for alleging that he, Vidal, was drunk and insulting during a visit to the Kennedy White House, Lee Radziwill, Jaqueline Kennedy's sister, refused to testify on Capote's behalf. Radziwill later said to the gossip columnist Liz Smith, "Oh, Liz, what do we care, they're just a couple of fags. They're disgusting." Whether the remark ever got back to Vidal is not known, but had it done so it would have reassured him that his sexuality had kept him permanently an outsider. The remark doesn't do much either to enhance the nobility of Princess Radziwill.

"I am exactly as I appear," Gore Vidal wrote. "There is no warm, lovable person inside. Beneath my cold exterior, once you break the ice, you will find cold water." He may well have been right.

Truman Capote was less charming than arresting. He got one's attention by saying outlandish things, usually in public places. On *The*

Johnny Carson Show he said the popular novelist Jackie Collins looked like nothing so much as "a truck driver in drag." Another time he called the novels of James Baldwin, by then dead and something of a sacred figure, not to be criticized, "balls-achingly boring." Capote must have expended considerable charm upon Babe Paley, Slim Keith, and other of the wealthy, fashionable women of Manhattan, the so-called "ladies who lunch," to win them over, but blew all the social capital he built up doing so when he published a portion of a never-to-be-completed novel based on them in *Esquire*. Charm will take one only so far, but in Truman Capote's case, not past serious indiscretions.

In modern times, gay charm first shows up in a major way in the works and even more in the personality—perhaps *persona* is the more precise word here—of Oscar Wilde (1854–1900). Wilde's distinctly gay charm showed up well before it was known that Wilde himself was gay; or perhaps it is more accurate to say one recognizes it unmistakably in the hindsight of his famous scandal. Had it not been for Wilde's litigation with the Marquis of Queensberry, whose son, Lord Alfred Douglas, was Wilde's lover, Oscar Wilde might never, at least in his lifetime, have been outed in one of the most famous trials of all time. Wilde sued the Marquis of Queensberry, for libel, after the latter left a card at the playwright's club that read, "For Oscar Wilde, posing sodomite." When it became clear in mid-trial that he was not going to win his case, Wilde dropped his suit, allowing the state to prosecute him. When it did so, in 1895, it found him guilty of "gross indecency" and sentenced him to two years imprisonment in Reading Gaol, from which he emerged a bankrupt and broken man, in which condition he died in Paris three years later at the age of forty-six.

Had Oscar Wilde not been outed in this sad way, would one today think of his writings as the product of a sensibility exhibiting, to a very high power, gay charm? He was a great showman, a self-promoter, posing for photographers in a green suit and cape holding a single lily ("One can never be overdressed or overeducated," he said). The form that gay charm takes in Wilde, both in his plays and in his conversation, is a sharp eye for seeing through social hypocrisy and a love of paradox.

Along with George Bernard Shaw, H. L. Mencken, and Dorothy Parker, Oscar Wilde is among the most quoted of modern writers; he is, one suspects, more quoted, certainly more quotable, than any of these other writers. The brilliance of his formulations is what makes his most much anthologized quotations memorable. Dorothy Parker attested to this when, in a bit of light verse, she wrote: "If, with the literate, I am/ Impelled to try an epigram,/I never seek to take the credit;/We all assume that Oscar said it."

Most of Oscar Wilde's most famous remarks are attacks on received opinions and conventional wisdom, strained through what I have been calling a gay sensibility. "Anyone who lives within his means suffers a lack of imagination," is one such example. "A little sincerity is a dangerous thing, and a great deal of it is absolutely fatal" is another. "True friends stab you in the front" is a nice reversal on enemies stabbing you in the back, and "Always forgive your enemies; nothing annoys them so much" is a nice play off the central Christian doctrine of forgiveness. The great sin for Wilde—no surprise here—is to be boring. He held that "there is only one thing in life worse than being talked about, and that is not being talked about."

Not being talked about was not usually Oscar Wilde's problem. He saw to that by his calculatedly outrageous behavior, though he was not everywhere esteemed. A surprising contemner of Wilde was Noël Coward, who himself exhibited gay charm to a very high power. The references to Wilde in Coward's diary are uniformly deflationary. "Am reading more of Oscar Wilde," Coward writes in 1946. "What a tiresome affected sod." At one point, working on *After the Ball*, his musical version of Wilde's *Lady Windermere's Fan*, Coward notes: "The more Coward we can get into the script and the more Wilde we can eliminate the happier we will be." Later he writes that

> *I have the Oscar Wilde letters and have come to the reluctant conclusion that he was one of the silliest, most conceited and unattractive characters that ever existed . . . It is extraordinary indeed that such a posing, arti-ficial old queen should have written one of the greatest comedies [Lady*

Windermere's Fan] in the English language. In my opinion it is the only thing of the least importance that he did write.

Noël Coward never expressed the least regret about his own homosexuality. Nor did he publicize it. He never mentions it in his published autobiographies, and he asked his official biographer not to mention it. The best defensive is strong offense, and Noël Coward's entire life may be said to have been a charm offensive. When late in life he was asked how he wished to be remembered, he answered, "By my charm." Charm for him meant being at all times interesting and amusing. "There's only one thing worse than being a dwarf," he said, "and that's being a boring dwarf." During a health campaign for slimness, he remarked that he'd "rather be fat than disgruntled," though he was never other than elegantly slender and generally cheerful. When he sounded the note of pessimism, he did so optimistically. His put-downs were never less than amusing. "Dear Randolph," he said of Winston Churchill's son, "so unspoiled by his great failure."

The theater critic Kenneth Tynan called Noël Coward "one of the brightest stars in the homosexual constellation that did so much to enliven the theatre between the wars." Tynan goes on to remark that Coward "invented the concept of cool . . . and made camp elegant. A master of understatement, he could make passion seem crude." Writing about Coward in 1973, the year of his death, Tynan claimed that "in fact his best work has not dated, by which I mean his most ephemeral."

Coward's charm turned up in his work and life both. The story is told of the five-year-old child of Laurence Olivier and Vivien Leigh, upon noting a male dog sniffing a female dog, asking what the animals were doing, and Coward responding: "The doggie in front has suddenly gone blind, and the one behind has very kindly offered to push him all the way to Dunstan Station." On another occasion, wearing a business, or lounge, suit, he walked into a party where every other man in the room was in white tie and tails. "Please," he announced, "no one need apologize for being overdressed."

Noël Coward was born in 1899 into that English no-man's-land known as the lower middle class. His father sold pianos. His mother, a stronger influence on him than his father, early sought a career in the theater for him. Public school and university were not in the cards for Noël, and he later averred that they "would probably have set me back years." The theater critic John Lahr suggests that Coward's charm covered his vulnerabilities, and being relatively low-born in highly class-conscious England may have been among them. If so, it was not for long, and vulnerable was the last thing anyone would have thought Noël Coward.

At the age of twenty-four, after a number of plays produced but indifferently received, he wrote, directed, and acted in *The Vortex,* a play about nymphomania and drug addiction, which was an enormous success and which in one stroke made him a coming man. At one point he had four plays staged simultaneously in London. "I was a highly publicized and irritatingly successful figure much in demand," he later wrote, [though] "the critical laurels that had been so confidently predicted for me in my twenties never graced my brow, and I was forced to console myself with the bitter palliative of box-office success. Which I enjoyed very much indeed."

Those last two sentences standing alone could serve as an exercise in irony-laced charm of the kind that was Coward's specialty. They also provide a mini-perspective on his view of the world: his disdain for the darkly high-brow in art, his pleasure at popular success, his playing at the sophisticate-cynic who believed there was no greater sin than being boring in public. "Subtlety, discretion, restraint, finesse, charm, elegance, good manners, talent, and glamour still enchant me," he wrote in his sixty-second year.

Coward quickly established in the public mind a self-portrait—very nearly a caricature—of himself as the man in the silken dressing gown, cigarette in long ivory holder, casually puffing out smoke and witticisms. As for his homosexuality, he never mentioned, let alone emphasized, it, for he felt to do so was boorish in the extreme, and anyhow he assumed everyone knew about it, apart perhaps, as he once noted, "a few old ladies in Worthing who don't know." Public acknowledgment of his sexual preference came only posthumously, when his diaries and a biography were published by his companion Graham Payn.

Noël Coward's charm in good part derived from his having found the world a continuously amusing place. This gave him a balance that served him well even in failure. He loathed gloom in others, and did not permit it for any length of time in himself. "How needlessly unhappy people make themselves and each other," he wrote. The titles of some of his own songs nicely reflect his bouncy pessimism: "Bad Times Just Around the Corner," "Don't Let's Be Beastly to the Hun," "I Wonder What Happened to Him" [About Englishmen cashiered out of the English Army in India for sexual high-jinx of one sort or another], "Don't Put Your Daughter on the Stage," "Mad Dogs and Englishmen," "Uncle Harry," "Why Do the Wrong People Travel," and others. These play in charming contrast to his songs of romance and of melancholy: "Sail Away," "I Wanted to Show You Paris," "This Is a Night for Lovers," and others, which do not hold up quite so well.

Common sense was a keynote in Noël Coward. Asked of his spiritual philosophy by a childhood friend, he had earlier written: "My philosophy is as simple as ever. I love smoking, drinking, moderate sexual intercourse on a diminishing scale, reading and writing (not arithmetic). I have a self-less absorption in the well-being of Noël Coward." Later he would give up drinking, noting, "I don't need it, I don't particularly like it, it makes me feel dull and heavy . . . it is fattening and boring, and so no more of it." Unlike Somerset Maugham, W. H. Auden, and other homosexual artists hostage to wretched lovers, he seemed to have had this aspect of his life well managed: "To me passionate love has always been like a tight shoe rubbing blisters on my Achilles heel." In his public so in his private life he never seemed other than in splendid control.

Noël Coward's amused view of the world, his great good common sense, his tactics for evading gloom all combined to endow him with his witty charm. Who else, after reading a memoir of life in a convent, could write, as did he, "It has strengthened my decision not to become a nun." Who else would have thought to call Las Vegas, where he appeared as a star performer late in his career, "Nescafe Society," or describe the actress Irene Handl as "just a large, breasty, good-hearted hunk of tangerine meat," or congratulate Gertrude Lawrence for a recent theatrical performance by offering her "a warm hand on your opening." On first seeing the Venus de Milo, he said, "It's only what's to be expected if you go on biting your nails."

The word *charm* crops up perhaps more than any other in *The Noël Coward Diaries* and in *The Letters of Noël Coward*. He finds Winston Churchill "ineffably charming." Irene Dunne is "so attractive and charming." So, too, Aneurin Bevan. Even the gangsters who ran Vegas in an earlier day he thinks "urbane and charming." He gives an audition of the score of a new musical he had written to eight ladies who organize theater-going parties, of which he notes: "As I despise and abominate theatre parties this went against the grain, but I persevered in the cause of true art and a healthy advance [of ticket sales] and charmed the shit out of them." Even charm, though, has its limits, and he writes of a disappointing off-Broadway production of his play *Conversation Piece* that it is done "pleasantly and gently and is, almost monotonously, charming."

What he cannot bear is pretension, and nowhere more than in the theater. The seriousness of Martha Graham makes him laugh. "She really is a bit long in the tooth now to go running about the stage on her knees, and even when she was young it wasn't a very sensible thing to do." Meeting Edward Albee he finds him "very intelligent but badly tainted with avant-garde, Beckett, etc. He talked quite a lot of cock." As for Beckett himself, he writes that, after reading *Waiting for Godot* carefully, "in my considered opinion it is pretentious gibberish, without any claim to importance whatsoever." Bertolt Brecht, Eugen Ionesco, and Harold Pinter do not come off any better. Arthur Miller he considers pompous and boring, with a "philosophy that is adolescent and sodden with self-pity," but then "the cruellest blow that life has dealt him is that he hasn't a grain of humor." Of John Osborne and the Angry Young Men, he claims not to understand why "the young generation, instead of knocking at the door, should bash the fuck out of it." He thought the Actors Studio a bad joke, and his advice to actors was, "Speak clearly, don't bump into people, and if you must have motivation, think of your pay packet on Friday."

Coward could even swear charmingly. When he meets the Irish roughhouse playwright Brendan Behan, he notes, "I think he was surprised that I could say cunt and fuck as easily and naturally as he could." These same and other similar words appear at various places in his letters and diaries, but are always used with amusing economy and in surprising ways. He goes to a showing of *The Prince and the Showgirl*, and remarks that "Marilyn Monroe looks very pretty and is charming at moments, but too much emphasis on tits and bottom." Citing the limitations of his tolerance for the too-lengthy company even of good friends, he writes: "The Almighty, whom I suspect of occasionally being on my side, realizes this with his infinite wisdom, and when he observes me going too far, giving out too much, and generally making a cunt of myself, he firmly knocks me out. I am most grateful to him."

Among modern artists, Noël Coward displayed the least distance between his art and his everyday self. He appears to have lived as if he were a character in one of his own plays. Between real life and stage, there was no seam; person and persona were one. Or if they truly weren't, he kept it beautifully hidden. "Style in everything demands discipline," he said. The figure he projected in both spheres was that of the sophisticated, elegant, utterly urbane gent, at home everywhere in the world. (He wrote an amusing song, titled "Home," on the subject.) "If you're a star, you should behave like one," he said. "I always have."

People were drawn to him, longed to be in his company, sometimes annoyingly so. He wrote in a letter to a friend:

People were greedy and predatory, and if you gave them a chance, they would steal unscrupulously the heart and soul out of you without really wanting to or meaning to. A little personality, a publicized name; a little entertainment value above the ordinary; and there they were, snatching and grabbing, clamorous in their demands, draining your strength to add a little fuel to their social bonfires.

His own social bonfire was always nicely stoked. He often found himself in the company of Winston Churchill and the king and queen of England and other social face cards of Europe; the most famous actors regularly shore up in what he once called "violently glamorous" surroundings, which pleased but daunted him not at all. He may have been born into the lower middle class, but, as Balzac avers, an artist is a prince, a natural aristocrat, and it so was for him.

Noël Coward's chief rule was the avoidance of boredom for others in whose company he found himself. He remarked of wit that it should be served as if it were "a glorious treat, like caviar, and not spread out like marmalade." His view of the public nicely encapsulates his social views generally: "Coax it, charm it, interest it, stimulate it, shock it now and again if you must, make it laugh, make it cry, make it think, but above all never, never, never bore the living hell out of it."

Along with a talent to amuse, Noël Coward had the gift of perspective. "My sense of my importance to the world is relatively small," he wrote in one of his autobiographies. "On the other hand, my sense of my importance to myself is tremendous." (A fine illustration, this, of living out F. Scott Fitzgerald's notion of keeping two contradictory ideas in one's mind at the same time!) He claimed to remain "extraordinarily unspoiled by my great success. As a matter of fact, I still am."

The test came when the golden faucet of endless success was turned off for him by a changed audience, indeed by a changed culture. After World War Two, his plays about the ideal, foolish, and often snobbish rich lost their appeal. He took even this with good grace, noting in his diary that in his younger days he "was tremendously keen to be a star and famous and successful; well, I have been successful for most of my life, and if at this late stage I have another series of resounding failures, I believe I could regard them with a certain equanimity."

This for the most part he did. He had another run as a stage performer, able to sell his sophisticated songs and wit, through the sheer power of charm, even to the coarse audiences in Las Vegas, where he was a great hit. What he took to be the dullness and boredom of the new age, though, remained unacceptable. England itself seemed to him done for: "Our history, except for stupid, squalid scandals, is over," he wrote in his diary. He thought the Beatles no more than "bad-mannered little shits." The aristocratic England, to which his charm and talent gained him entry, was on the way out. He spoke of feeling "a core of sadness about England, a sadness mixed with a sort of desolate irritation that a country and a people so rich in tradition and achievement should betray itself and what it stands for by so whole-heartedly submitting to foolish government, natural laziness, woolly thinking, and above all the new religion of mediocrity."

Still, Noël Coward claimed to look back on his life "not in anger [but] rather I look back in pleasure and amusement." In the end he admired "courage and humor more than any other qualities." If he also admired celebrity, and was not displeased to have been a celebrity himself for most of his life, it was those celebrities with genuine achievement behind them, such as Somerset Maugham and Rebecca West, whom he truly admired and of whom he must, rightly, himself be considered one.

Following an afternoon with the eighty-three-year-old Somerset Maugham, Coward drove home "in the evening sunlight feeling happy and stimulated and deeply impressed by the charm of old age when it is allied to health and intelligence." Yet the prospect of too long a life was not one that appealed to him. Four years before his actual death in 1973, he wrote: "It is possible that I might stagger on to the nineties, which mean nearly another quarter of a century. I cannot say that I find this prospect very alluring. I would prefer Fate allow me to go to sleep when it's my proper bedtime. I never have been one for staying up too late." Noël Coward departed the planet at the age of seventy-four, easily the most charming man of his day and one of the most charming human beings, straight or gay, transgendered or hermaphroditic, two or more legged, in the twentieth century.

CHAPTER XI

The Charmingest Generation

IN 2001 THE NEWSCASTER TOM BROKAW WROTE A BOOK CALLED *THE GREAT-est Generation*, by which he meant those who fought in World War Two. Whether he was right about this or not—the generation of the founding fathers, after all, was not without its greatness either—is arguable. Less arguable is that no generation was more charming than that comprising the great African-American jazz and swing musicians who came onto the public stage in the 1920s and '30s.

Grace under pressure was the way Ernest Hemingway defined courage. The black jazz and swing musicians took things a step further and in an often hostile environment, they performed with insouciance, suavity, and wit. To their artistry they brought the extra ingredient of charm. Charm displayed under such exigent social conditions is itself a form of courage.

The generation of African-American musicians I have in mind is the pre-hard-drug generation, whose key figures were Joe Oliver, Fats Waller, Willie Smith, Eubie Blake, Cab Calloway, Errol Gardner, Bessie Smith, Lionel Hampton, Count Basie, Art Tatum, Ella Fitzgerald, and above all Louis Armstrong and Duke Ellington. The jazz musicians who came after them—Charlie Parker, John Coltrane, Billie Holiday, Miles Davis, Dizzy Gillespie—advanced the art of jazz, but charm was not their specialty. Cool, with all its implied distancing of oneself from human contact, was. Drugs may have revealed another world to them, deepening and darkening their music, but drugs also often left many of them snarly and snarky, their music dark, their spirits down. The charmingest generation, while scarcely

Rotarian in its optimism, was nonetheless dedicated to delivering happiness through its music and through the personalities of many of its members.

Louis Armstrong and Duke Ellington are two men who could scarcely have been more unlike—in background, outlook, style—yet each flourished and left his lasting impress on American culture through a combination of musical genius and very different kinds of charm. Extraordinary as was the talent of both men, each viewed himself as essentially an entertainer—though neither argued when others called them geniuses—and as entertainers their charm went a long way to establishing their fame.

Edward Kennedy Ellington was born into the black middle class in Washington DC, Louis Armstrong was born in the slums of New Orleans. Ellington's father worked as first a driver then a butler for a wealthy white Washington, DC, physician. His mother was a high-school graduate—no small accomplishment for a black female of that era—a beautiful woman of natural refinement. Armstrong's mother worked as a prostitute in New Orleans' bordello quarter; his father deserted him and his sister early in their lives. Ellington's mother repeatedly told him that he was "blessed." (A man certain of his mother's love, Freud claimed, was a conqueror.) He was, as he allowed, "pampered and spoiled rotten by all the women in the [extended] family." As his nickname implies, Ellington came across as slightly distant and aristocratic.

Louis Armstrong was left to fend for himself from an early age. As a young boy, he worked with a Jewish family named Karnofsky, delivering coal to whorehouses, and bringing his wages home to his mother. His style was familiar, down-home. He called everyone Pops; he possessed one of the great natural smiles and over the years acquired a gravelly voice nicely attuned to conveying the good humor that angry blacks would mistakenly contemn as Uncle Tom.

Duke and Satchmo—the first nickname deriving from Ellington's elegance of manner, the second from Armstrong's large, or satchel mouth—the one a gifted piano player and composer, the other unsurpassed on the trumpet and a magnificent jazz and popular singer, the two combined may have brought more musical pleasure than any other performers in the history of our country. And they did it during a time when Negroes, as African Americans then were called, were denied the most basic rights.

If later generations wanted clear definitions of charm, these two men, in their different ways, provided it not only in their music and manner but in the examples of their own lives.

Although Louis Armstrong was born in New Orleans and Duke Ellington in Washington, DC, each man had to take to the road to establish himself: Armstrong to Chicago, where he played trumpet in the band of Joe "King" Oliver, Ellington to New York, where he organized his first bands to play at the Cotton Club in Harlem. During the 1960s and '70s both men were given a bad rap for being insufficiently political, though the FBI kept a dossier on Ellington for his very tenuous connection with popular front groups in the 1940s and '50s. Armstrong, in later life, was not above scolding fellow blacks for not working together to improve the standing and condition of the race. Somehow, though, all that seemed secondary, if not tertiary and beyond, next to the deep delight they brought through their music and personal charm. "I am dedicated," said Louis Armstrong, "to the pursuit of happiness." He, and Duke Ellington along with him, not only pursued it but captured it and purveyed it, to the great and everlasting delight of all.

Of Louis Armstrong, Bing Crosby said: "I never met anybody that didn't love him that ever saw him work or ever has encountered him, had any connection or business with him." Part of Armstrong's immense charm was in his ability to treat everyone alike. Playing a command performance in London for King George V, who apparently knew a lot about popular music, he motioned toward the royal box and said, "This one's for you, Rex," and went into his rendition of "You Rascal You." When in Rome, the normally chilling Pope Pius XII asked Armstrong if he and his wife had any children, to which he answered: "No, Daddy, but we're working on it." As he called everyone Pops, so Pops became the name by which everyone came to know him. Tallulah Bankhead, as we have seen a tough critic of human personality, said of Armstrong: "I love to talk to him because of his basic sincerity and his very original gift of expression. He uses words like he strings notes together—artistically and vividly."

Everyone who ever saw Louis Armstrong perform on stage seems to have remembered it. A great showman, "his personality," as his biographer Terry Teachout writes "was as compelling as his artistry." Of that showmanship, the jazz critic Whitney Balliett wrote: "Armstrong's stage presence—a heady and steadily revolving mixture of thousand-watt teeth, marbling eyes, rumbling asides, infectious laughter, and barreling gait—is as endearing a spectacle as we have had on the American stage." Everyone who knew him reports that Louis Armstrong was much the same on and off stage. "They know I'm there," he said, "in the cause of happiness."

Armstrong was nonpareil in two lines. He was probably the greatest trumpet player of all time. Dizzy Gillespie, Miles Davis, later Wynton Marsalis, his peers on the trumpet if he may be said to have had peers, all recognized his supremacy on the instrument. He was, according to Whitney Balliett, the first jazz soloist. The composer and critic Virgil Thomson wrote of his playing that "his style of improvisation would seem to have combined the highest reaches of instrumental virtuosity with the most tensely disciplined melodic structure and the most spontaneous emotional expression, all of which in one man you must admit to be pretty rare." As a musician, he was a man with little in the way of disruptive egotism. Dexter Gordon, Milt Hinton, and other great jazz musicians remarked on what a delight it was to play with him.

Armstrong never would have attained the fame he did if he hadn't also sung. He acquired his famous gravelly voice through a hoarseness that first came on in his early days when he played in bands on Mississippi river boats. Fletcher Henderson described it as "that big fish horn voice of his." Terry Teachout says, rightly, that "he sang with a charm that only a critic could resist." He could take thin, or even dopily sentimental songs— "Hello, Dolly," or "It's a Wonderful World"—and by sheer force of style make them irresistible. He sometimes mumbled or otherwise bungled the lyrics, even on his recordings, but it didn't seem to matter. He could also lightly mock an inane song, the way Fats Waller did, while simultaneously bringing pleasure singing it. He invented jazz singing. He was not the first to sing scat, but the first to turn it into an art.

Louis Armstrong mated musical genius with personal charm in a manner warm, familiar, ultimately charming. Duke Ellington, pianist, orchestrator, band leader, composer, was, in contrast, more distant yet never cold. No biographer yet has captured Ellington's interior life, or anything close to it. Perhaps he lacked one. He was a musician full-time, even in his sleep, where new melodies came to him as they did anywhere else he might be.

If Louis Armstrong could easily charm you, more likely you would feel the need to charm Duke Ellington, from whom the charm of one of nature's noblemen seemed to pour. Sonny Greer, the first drummer in the Ellington band, called him "the Prince of Wale." Bill Berry, a cornetist with the Ellington orchestra, said: "Ellington was the kind of guy when he walked into a room a light went on. Armstrong was like that, too. Even if somebody didn't know who they were they can feel this magnetism." The very titles of Duke Ellington's songs and musical compositions exude charm: "Prelude to a Kiss," "Sophisticated Lady," "Mood Indigo," "In My Solitude," "Subtle Lament," "Perdido," "If It Ain't Got That Swing It Don't Mean A Thing." He gave jazz elegance.

When Ellington walked the streets of New York, strangers were delighted to greet him. As Armstrong called everyone Pops, Ellington called most people Babe. He was one of those men on whom all clothes looked good. He put together surprising but always effective color combinations. All his suits, shirts, shoes, hats, even his male cologne were custom made. "Ellington dresses sleekly, but without dandaism," Kenneth Tynan noted. Even in work clothes—uncreased trousers, loose sweaters—his natural elegance shone through. The heavy bags under his eyes—genuine two-suiters—a sign of aging on anyone else on him seemed a nice touch. Late in life he took to wearing a pigtail, and may have been the only man in the twentieth century who could bring it off without looking a schmuck. He didn't have to be mindful of fashion; he was one of those people who set fashion. In clothes as in music and just about everything else, he was his own man, as are all men and women of genuine charm.

Ellington was a florid flatterer of women, though he didn't require it, for women adored him even without the flattery. He remained married to the same woman all his days, but was, as was Louis Armstrong, a player. On the road, up on the bandstand, the cynosure of everyone in the room, it would have been difficult not to be. Rex Stewart, for many years the cornetist in the Ellington band, remarked: "Many of the lovely ladies upon whom Duke cast an approving eye, and then heaped exquisite compliments have succumbed. The number of [his] conquests is uncountable."

An old joke has it that the toughest thing for basketball players in the NBA is not smiling when kissing one's wife good-bye before going off on a road trip. Ellington would have got the joke.

Yet women never seemed at the center of Duke Ellington's life. His complex musical life took up most of his available oxygen. Ellington composed through his orchestra. Other composers, classical and jazz, might compose on their piano and on notepads, but Ellington began with melodies rattling round in his head that he tried out on the magnificent musicians in his orchestra; not infrequently, he picked up the melody in something one or another of his all-star cast of musicians did during a riff. "My band is my instrument," he said. These musicians—some of the most famous among them over the years were Johnny Hodges, Sonny Greer, Cootie Williams, Sidney Bechet, Clark Terry, Shorty Baker, and Paul Gonsalves—could be quite as eccentric as Ellington; no small part of his charm was spent in manipulating them to do musically exactly as he wished. "He knew how to get whatever he wanted," the bassist Aaron Bell said, "and he always knew what he wanted." In Billy Strayhorn he found a perfect complement to his own talent for composition and arranging.

John Hammond, the musical producer and talent scout, called Duke Ellington "one of the most completely charming [men] I have ever come across. His disposition is without rival among artists, for he has never been known to lose his temper or do conscious ill to anyone." Such was his charm that he even turned ostensible setbacks into occasions for quiet wit. When he was denied a Pulitzer Prize for music in 1965 after having been nominated for it by the prize committee, he said: "Fate is being kind to me. Fates doesn't want me to be too famous too young." (He was then sixty-six years old.) The prizes and awards came later, and in abundance. Not that he needed them. He always had the greatest—the only serious prize—admiration of his peers: Percy Grainger and Leopold Stokowski thought well of his music, and Igor Stravinsky often went to the Cotton Club in Harlem when Ellington and his band played there.

In a brief essay called "Homage to Duke Ellington," Ralph Ellison, who in *Invisible Man* wrote the subtlest of all African-American novels, best put the effect of Duke Ellington's charm, both personal and musical.

To how many thousands has he brought definitions of what it should mean to be young and alive and American? Yes, and to how many has he given a sense of personal elegance and personal style? A sense of possibility? And who, seeing and hearing Ellington and his marvelous band, hasn't been moved to wonder at the mysterious, unanalyzed character of the Negro American—and at the white American's inescapable Negro-ness.

Ellington and the musicians in his band, Ellison went on to say, provided the grandest of masculine figures for young black men to identify with. "Where, in the white community, in *any* white community, could there have been found images, examples such as these? Who were so worldly, who so elegant, who so mockingly creative? Who so skilled at their given trade, and who treated the social limitations placed in their paths with greater disdain?"

By "social limitations placed in their paths" Ralph Ellison of course meant the strict legal and social prejudice against blacks in the early and middle years of Louis Armstrong's and Duke Ellington's careers. Ellington did the best he could to avert the uglier aspects of racial segregation. He and his band traveled in their own railroad cars, in which they slept and took their meals. "We never let ourselves be put in a position of disrespect," he said.

Louis Armstrong was less well situated in this regard, and stayed in third-class black accommodations in the South and usually traveled hard miles by bus. Of Jim Crow, Ellington said: "You have to try not to think about it, or you'll knock yourself out." Louis Armstrong took to heart the advice he received from Joe "King" Oliver, which was "to learn never to wear the trouble on your face."

In later years both Ellington and Armstrong were criticized by angry young blacks for being insufficiently political. James Baldwin, Miles Davis, the young Dizzy Gillespie, and Sammy Davis Jr. accused Armstrong, in being willing to play before Southern audiences, of being the entertainment version of an Uncle Tom. A bum rap, this. In fact, Louis Armstrong helped opened up both radio and movies for black entertainers. When President Eisenhower at first refused to send federal troops to help integrate Central High School in Little Rock, Arkansas, Armstrong publicly called Eisenhower "two-faced" and "gutless." He threatened to cancel his State Department tour of Europe on the grounds that his own country, in its treatment of black children in the South, was an embarrassment that he couldn't be expected to defend while abroad.

Ellington felt straight-out protest against Jim Crow laws beside the point, and thought economic pressure more effective in bringing about social change. (He turned out to be half right about this; it was a combination of the two that was needed.) Work not politics was Ellington's first order of business, and no one was more emphatic about the origins and meaning and ultimately political content of his life's work than Duke Ellington. "Naturally," he said, "my own race is closest to my own heart, and it is in the musical idiom of that race that I find my most natural expression. Just now we're calling it swing . . . but it all adds up to a lot of satisfaction at sharing in the achievement of the Negro race."

At the same time, Ellington and Armstrong were both critical of their own race, Armstrong more openly than Ellington. Mercer Ellington, Duke's son, claimed that his father's early composition "Black, Brown and Beige" was written in subtle protest against prejudice within African-American society, which placed a higher valuation on lighter skin. "As a whole," Mercer Ellington said, "the race wanted recognition and equal rights, and yet within themselves they restricted each other."

In one of his autobiographies, Armstrong took after the blacks for being envious and rivalrous within themselves. He compared them unfavorably with the Jews—based in part on his firsthand experience with the Karnofsky family in New Orleans—who supported one another, and always aided the downtrodden and defeated among their co-religionists. Armstrong's own manager, Joe Glaser, a thuggish character with Mafia connections in Chicago, was also Jewish.

Duke Ellington and Louis Armstrong admired each other immensely. Ellington said Armstrong "is also a great personality, we say also great, not because he is lesser, but because we cannot think of further terms. Unless possibly to say he is the heroic-size standard in trumpet. He is also a brilliant comedian." At Louis Armstrong's funeral, Ellington said of him: "He was born poor, died rich, and never hurt anyone along the way."

Armstrong felt singing and playing with the Ellington orchestra inspiring, and some of his best performances were done with Ellington, singing and playing music that Duke had composed. When they worked together, there was no conflict between them, no clash of temperament or authority, but just two great professionals working in tandem. Some of the best evidence of this is available on a CD called *Louis Armstrong, Duke Ellington, The Great Summit,* in which Louis Armstrong sings several of Duke Ellington's greatest songs and plays trumpet along with the orchestra. Great, splendid, magnificent stuff, it also happens to be, at no extra charge, utterly charming.

CHAPTER XII

Now for Someone Completely Charming

IN HIS *HISTORY OF GREEK CULTURE*, JACOB BURKHARDT, DISCUSSING THE complex relationship between Athens and Syracuse, takes up the story of Dion (408–354 BCE), friend of Plato and brother-in-law and chief adviser of the Syracusan tyrant Dionysius I. Burckhardt writes: "At the suggestion of Plato, he [Dion] associated with Plato's nephew Speusippus and deliberately cultivated charm and a pleasing character." What caught my attention, of course, was the phrase "deliberately cultivated charm." I believe I know how to cultivate the rudiments of pleasing, but about charm I am much less certain.

In his book *Youth* Leo Tolstoy writes that in his late adolescence he strove for "a general perfection"—"a desire to be better not in my own eyes or those of God but a desire to be better in the eyes of other men . . . a desire to be stronger than others, that is to say, more famous, more important, richer." He wished above all to be *comme il faut*. The ways to become stronger, famous, important, rich, *comme il faut* are, if not easy, nonetheless fairly clear. The way to become charming is not. At the court of Louis XIV, a school was founded for the daughters of impoverished noblemen called Saint-Cyr-l'École, which was the first of the charm schools. In it young women's personalities were shaped and polished, readying them to perform in aristocratic society and thereby to capture admirable husbands. In the middle of the past century, there were finishing, or charm, schools, instructing young women on poise, conversation, posture—young women walking with books balanced atop their heads was in those days a standard charm-school photo and symbol—manners, and makeup. This, though, is scarcely charm in the sense most people understand the word.

Imagine a person—a man in this instance—without fame or great wealth, who decides he wishes to acquire charm. How might he go about it? To begin with, he would need to be imbued with certain fundamental skills. He would require an elementary sense of those he was talking to, and what is likely to appeal to them. Can this be learned? Or is this an instinctive skill, which one either has or can never acquire? Bores obviously don't have it, and boors don't care about it. The person setting out to charm the company he finds himself in must know what interests these people, what they are likely to find amusing, what is both within and beyond the bounds of their sense of decorum. This sense of decorum can of course vary widely, from people who find the least profanity objectionable to others who aren't put off by a raucous joke with fellatio as its subject.

Sensing one's company is the first step, setting out to please without dominating it is the more difficult second step on the path to charm. And to what degree to please them—from mildly amusing to absolutely delighting them—is yet another question. This of course supposing that one has the skill, talent, social ammunition to amuse (however mildly), let alone to delight. What might this include? Fascinating anecdotes, clever puns, perfectly told jokes, dazzling repartee, delicately applied name-dropping? All this, and more, but none of it seeming forced or in any way crudely, obviously meant to charm.

In a life of any modest length, anecdotes build up, one has had experiences worth recounting, observations worth making, favorite jokes one has stored up. The charming person knows how to deploy such material, to serve it, so to say, in a pleasing presentation. In the realm of charm, presentation is crucial. The great mistake is to force the anecdote or the joke into conversation, however inherently interesting or amusing it might be. Part of the subtlety entailed in charming is not to seem to want to charm, but instead merely, casually, simply to be charming. To seem to want to charm is to have lost all hope of being charming. No show of strain, of preparation, of neediness, of longing for acceptance must emerge. A strong element of the casual is part of the equipage of charm: Charm must always seem unforced, natural, free, and easy.

Charm must also be integrated into the charming person's personality. One can, I suppose, be charming sometimes, or even part-time. But charm is pretty much a full-time job. This sounds onerous. Yet it may well be that the truly charming person doesn't have to think of any of the attributes of charm or how best to display them. He already knows, and he knows because, mirabile dictu, he *is* charming, normally, naturally, invariably charming. He can't be uncharming even if he tried.

If one isn't by nature such a person, how can one go about turning oneself, cultivating oneself, à la Dion of Syracuse, into one? No one, after all, is born with charm. Some people, though, seem to attain it effortlessly, while for others, most others, it is unattainable. Did the charming at some point note their potential and work at developing it—testing, through trial and observation, what worked and what didn't? Did they, like boy athletes, find models in professionals whose style they copied, if not wholly at least in part, taking this from one model and other things from others, finally forging a unique charm of their own? Is not all fully formed charm a potpourri of a similar kind, formed from models discovered in the movies, from books, from admirably charming persons one has encountered in one's own social experiences?

Perhaps the first thing a person who sets out to be charming needs to keep in mind is the distinctions between being charming and being flattering and between charming and being amusing merely. Flattery, in a base definition, is telling a person what he wants to hear. This may make one seem charming to the person being flattered but to everyone else it is less charming than sycophantic and hence ignoble. Flattery, no doubt, is an art form of its own, with quite as many modes and variations as are possible on the clarinet, but it has nothing to do with charm, except perhaps that subtle charm can flatter the intelligence of its audience.

A charming person is often amusing, but amusement is only a minor aspect of charm. The comedian Henny Youngman was amusing, so, too, were Rodney Dangerfield and Jackie Mason, but none of them qualifies as charming. True, a charming person is unlikely to be humorless, but he need not be notably funny. There is the charm of suavity, of elegant language, of beautiful manners subtly displayed. The main point of charm, I have come to believe, is to bring delight. An odd word, *delight*, suggesting lighting things up, making them brighter.

I suspect that the only way to acquire charm is to study with some care models of charm one has encountered in life, literature, or anywhere else. I should like to pause here, then, to describe a person I've never met but whom over the years I've read and read about and whom I consider a superior model of charm. That person is the English writer and caricaturist Max Beerbohm (1872–1956). Not a household name, Max Beerbohm's, I realize, but most people who have read his essays, or viewed his caricatures, or knew him while he lived would, there can be little doubt, have deemed him charming.

If you haven't before now heard of Max Beerbohm, not to worry, he would have been neither surprised nor much concerned about your not knowing of him. Quite the reverse; it might even have pleased him. Early in S. N. Behrman's book *Portrait of Max,* he, Beerbohm, brings out a royalty statement from his American publishers showing how few copies of his books were sold. I write "how few," but the royalty statement showed, Behrman reports, "an unbroken column of zeros. 'Not one copy!' crowed Max in triumph. 'Not One.' It was an understandable paean from a man who cherishes privacy."

Max Beerbohm wrote essays, a fantasy novel about a dazzlingly beautiful girl at Oxford (*Zuleika Dobson*), a single book of short stories (*Seven Men and Two Others*), and drama criticism. He also drew scores of caricatures of contemporary writers, artists, and politicians. All this work had his inimitable touch; all could only have been written or drawn by him. Oscar Wilde noted that Beerbohm had a style "like a silver dagger." His personality was marked in all he produced, all he said. "In every art," Max Beerbohm wrote, apropos of the music-hall performer Dan Leno, "personality is the paramount thing, and without it artistry goes for little." The hallmark of his own personality was a subtle intimacy that never became cloying, never lapsed into bad taste.

To dine with Max, said Edith Wharton, "was like suddenly growing wings." Utterly unselfish in conversation, with other people his watchword was "tell me." His dear friend Will Rothstein said that Max, "who charms everyone, found everyone charming. And how quickly he discovers the essence of each personality." Max himself said that "with a little good will one can always find something impressive in anybody."

During World War Two, Max returned to England from his home in Rapallo, in Italy, and gave BBC broadcasts that had a wide, even a vast, audience. "It is odd that one of the least popular writers in the world should have become, next to Winston Churchill, the most popular broadcaster in England during the most critical moment in its history," Behrman wrote. When listening to Max Beerbohm's wartime broadcasts, Rebecca West recalled feeling "that I was listening to the voice of the last civilized man on earth."

One of Max Beerbohm's first tenets was that to take oneself too seriously was a form of lunacy. "Only the insane take themselves quite seriously," he said. One had an obligation to recognize one's limitations. George Bernard Shaw, Rudyard Kipling, D. H. Lawrence among his contemporaries, may be said to have suffered from what he called "a sublimity of earnestness," or lack of humor, at least about themselves. "Poor D. H. Lawrence," he remarked. "He never realized, don't you know—he never suspected that to be stark, staring mad is something of a handicap to a writer." Of T. E. Lawrence's apparently wretched translation of the *Odyssey*, Max Beerbohm wrote: "I would rather not have been that translator than have driven the Turks out of Arabia."

Max Beerbohm suspected genius and was opposed to giantism in the arts; in his eyes all geniuses were guilty until proven innocent, and few were so proven. His own predilection was for the small scale. E. M. Forster wrote that, Goethe apart, all geniuses were in some sense stupid. Even with Goethe Max found fault: "But a man whose career was glorious without intermission, decade after decade, does sorely try our patience," he wrote. He said of Yeats that in reading him he felt "rather uncomfortable, as though I had submitted myself to a mesmerist who somehow didn't mesmerise me." Conversely he noted of the poetry of Robert Graves that his "joy in him is not diminished because he is intelligible." He mocked the discovery in England through the translations of Constance Garnett of the great nineteenth-century Russian novelists, and wrote a parody called "Kolniyatsch" about the reception of a Dostoyevsky-like novelist he invented. The name *Kolyniyatsch* derives from "Colony Hatch," a once-famous English mental asylum, and my favorite line in the parody is "The promised biography of the murdered grandmother is eagerly awaited by all who take—and which of us does *not* take—a breathless interest in Kolniyatschiana." He thought Dante, in the bitterness of his exile, would have made a poor houseguest, and an even worse host. He referred to Tolstoy and Nietzsche as "inspired asses." In an essay called "A Clergyman," he takes the side of an unnamed clergyman whom Samuel Johnson, in Boswell's *Life of Johnson*, puts down as one would flick a fly off one's shoulder. "My heart goes out to the poor dear clergyman exclusively," he wrote, though in later life he, Max, came round to admire Samuel Johnson.

Upon meeting Beerbohm, Edmund Wilson, the formidable American literary critic, was much impressed by his self-confidence. "He's quite sure of himself. He knows the value of what he has done, both as a writer and as an artist." Yet, Wilson went to note, he also seemed to be quite without ambition or envy of any kind. Nor was there anything the least pretentious about him. Quite the reverse. Max confessed to his inability to read philosophy when it was in the least abstract, but then, he added, "I suffer from a strong suspicion that things in general cannot be accounted for through any formula or set of formulae, and that any one philosophy, howsoever new, is no better than another." He held that no foreign speaker—himself above all—ever mastered speaking French, and the palm in this hopeless enterprise went to the person who spoke it, displaying the least hesitation, with the greatest confidence.

Max had a natural detachment. This was a component of his self-sufficiency. He was pleased to be in agreeable company but didn't require it, solitude and self-enjoyment providing pleasure enough. He drew and wrote as if for himself, but in a way that strangers could nonetheless enjoy. Outwardly social, he was inwardly reflective. "I have the power of getting out of myself," he said. "That is a very useful power." Violet Schiff, a friend, noted his respect for women, his kindness to servants; she also concluded that, while he was well aware of what the world valued—money, fame, success of various kinds—he was himself indifferent to them.

This detachment served his charm well. He never attempted to dominate conversation. He had no need to do so. He had command of an ornate but always precise vocabulary in which such words as *agororpho-bious* and *pleasaunces* turn up. His oblique observations brought laughter. "It is Bertrand Russell's saving grace that he isn't a woman," he said. "As a woman he would have been intolerable." Just so, even though one isn't quite certain why that remark is both accurate and funny. "I *must* read *The Golden Bowl*—and yet I shan't," he wrote. He allows that rich men were often bright and good, yet "I have always felt they would have been brighter and better still on moderate means." As for intellectual fashions: "It distresses me," he wrote, "this failure to keep pace with the leaders of thought as they pass into oblivion." His single-sentence refutation of Freudianism cannot be topped: "They were a tense and peculiar family, the Oedipuses, weren't they?"

Max Beerbohm's friend Will Rothstein noted his early polish and soundness of judgment. David Cecil, Beerbohm's biographer, wrote that he seemed to have skipped adolescence, and went directly from childhood to maturity. Oscar Wilde said that he "had the gift of perpetual old age." The mystical and high-flown, in art and in life, held no interest for him. He was not least amusing about his own gifts. "I have no time to write more," he noted in a letter to his friend Rothstein, "lest I lapse into brilliancy." His older brother, the famous-in-his-day actor Herbert Beerbohm Tree once told him "I can stand any amount of flattery—if only it is fulsome enough." To which Max replied: "Oh, I make no conditions of any sort."

"All social life is founded on certain carefully fostered illusions," Max Beerbohm wrote. "Let us respect them. It is through them alone that men can keep out of mischief." He also noted that "candor is only good when it reveals good actions and good sentiments and that, when it reveals evil, it is evil itself." Max himself never showed hostility, never gossiped in a destructive way. He was content to be among life's onlookers, the nicely turned out fellow there on the sidelines, a glass of wine in hand, enjoying his own ironic observations. G. K. Chesterton said of Max that "he seems to me more modest and realistic about himself than about anything else," adding that "he does not indulge in the base idolatry of believing in himself."

Max Beerbohm considered himself an essayist, in his literary and his non-literary life. Which is another way of saying that he never thought himself a major player, shimmering with significance. He was without egotism, literary or social. "Some people are born to lift heavy weights," he wrote. "Some people are born to juggle golden balls." He knew himself to be among the jugglers—that is, among the charmers, at least as a writer and draughtsman. He would never have been so vain as to consider himself socially charming, which he indubitably was.

So much so that Max began to feel the strain of performing socially, to attend to "the humble, arduous process of making myself agreeable." David Cecil writes that "the very fact that he had so high a reputation for agreeableness made his life more of an effort: for it meant he felt bound to try to live up to it." In time this began to wear on him. "I can repay hospitality," he wrote, "only by strict attention to the humble, arduous process of making myself agreeable. When I go up to dress for dinner, I always have a strong impulse to go to bed and sleep off my fatigue . . ."

Boredom with social pressure of this kind contributed to Max Beerbohm's moving, with his wife, the American actress Florence Kahn, to Rapallo in 1910 when he was thirty-eight, taking, in effect, early retirement. He would live there forty-five years longer, returning to England only during the World War Two years, dying at Rapallo at eighty-three. He never bothered to learn Italian, nor left the Villino, as his villa was called, apart from walking down to the sea to bathe in summer. Working at his drawings and occasional essays, he was content within himself. He lived socially off guests passing through. "People come to see me," he told the English writer Christopher Sykes, "either on the way from [Somerset] Maugham [at Cap Ferrat] to [Bernard] Berenson [at Villa I Tatti, outside Florence], or on the way to Maugham from Berenson. I am a way station." Ezra Pound also lived in Rapallo, but, obstreperous fellow that he was, not to speak of his later conversion to Italian fascism, holding only strong views that he wished to impose on all, Pound, one might say, was the anti-Max, and Beerbohm pretty much steered clear of him.

If Max Beerbohm suspected genius, and eschewed gigantism generally—when S. N. Behrman suggested his works might fit nicely into a single Modern Library Giant volume, Max replied that, were this to happen, "I should have to change my wardrobe"—if he specialized in the light and amusing, he was nonetheless far from insignificant and trivial. Within his seemingly light essays and presumably tossed-off drawings, a mature and serious vision shone through. This vision is partially captured in a brief essay he wrote, fewer than eight short pages, called "Something Defeasible," about a small boy building a cottage out of sand and his pleasure in seeing it destroyed by the incoming tide. "It was the boy's own enthusiasm that made me feel, as never before, how deep-rooted in the human breast the love of destruction, of mere destruction, is." About to proceed from this observation to dark thoughts about the human psyche and the fate of England, Max Beerbohm pulls back, explaining his decision and ending by writing "for I wished to be happy while I might."

"For I wished to be happy while I might"—what a perfect motto for those who find life delightful and through their own charm bring delight to others!

As for what Dion learned about becoming charming from Plato's nephew Speusippus, Jacob Burckhardt is silent. It was probably little more than I have learned from Max Beerbohm or you from people who seem to you models of charm. No one finally teaches charm, nor can charm be carefully copied without seeming stale and flat. Fortunately, though, there have been men and women around who can show the rest of us what it looks like, and that is no small thing.

PART THREE

Chapter XIII

Charm in the Age of the Therapeutic

As I mentioned, once I set to work on this book I would occasionally ask friends and acquaintances to name five people currently in public
life they thought charming. By public life I meant people in politics, show
business, sports, the arts. The results, invariably, were disappointing. No
one came up with five names; many failed to come up with any names at
all. Those that came up with a name or two did so only with some hesitation. The names that did arise—Steve Martin, Oprah Winfrey, Princess
Diana, Bill Murray, Barack Obama—were all disputable, rather easily so.
None garnered anything like the same consensus of approval as candidates
for charm as the men and women on the scene a generation or two ago.
There must, I concluded, be a paucity of charming people about just now.
But why?

No one thought to name any of the plethora of late-night talk-show
hosts, whose only claim on the job, one would once have thought, would
have been their charm. No news anchormen or anchorwomen were
named. No one came up with a movie star or singer. No athletes, no
comedians, no writers or painters or musicians, none were named. Did I
ask the wrong people? Should I have asked more young (thirty and under)
people about their candidates for charming? Somehow, I don't think it
would have mattered. Is it possible that charm itself is not a contemporary
ideal? Why should there be so few charming people currently on the
American—and I suspect also on the European—scene? If I am correct
about there in fact being so few charming people in public life, why is this
so, how did it come about, what are its consequences?

I am a man of *d'un âge certain,* as the French say, or an *alte kocker,* as the Jews say, and it could be that I am missing out on more than one generation of charming men and women, whose youth and my own taste put out of my ken. Somehow, though, I rather doubt it. When I think of the Mills Brothers or Nat King Cole and compare them with current-day rappers, Jay-Z, say, or LL Cool J, in the realm of charm there is no contest, with the mature suavity of the former towering about the deliberate abrasiveness and in-your-face profanity and racial anger, of the latter. When I think of Bing Crosby, Frank Sinatra, and Johnny Mercer and the urbanity they put into the adult lyrics of the songs they sang and compare them with Mick Jagger or Elton John (the former a great-grandfather, both men knighted) and their essentially childish songs and Jagger's bumps and grinds and John's banging away on his piano, a Liberace in sunglasses, again, no contest. I don't care in the least for Madonna, though I find Lady Gaga's hyper showbiz glitz act mildly amusing, and I enjoy Adele. But without hesitation I'd take Jo Stafford and Ella Fitzgerald over all of them or any other contemporary female singer now performing. I could go on, but you will have got my drift.

In defense of my belief that this is not mere old guy's crankiness on my part, I would argue that there is something about the current age that is, if not outright anti-charm, not especially partial to charm as an ideal. In the current day, to be or seem authentic is clearly more important than to be or seem winning; to be or seem honest more important than to be or seem gracious. To do one's own thing (a phrase from the 1960s) better than to worry about other people's things, which is to say, their feelings and reactions. Charm operates exclusively in the realm of the social; while charming people are invariably unique, each like no other, authenticity, honesty, doing one's own thing are all of them individual, or personal, rather than social goals.

In recent decades, perhaps beginning as early as the early 1960s, the emphasis on life has been more and more on the individual, on the Big First Person, I, Me, Mine Truly. Tom Wolfe called the 1970s "The Me Decade," though the "Me" part surely didn't end with the decade itself. When Wolfe first published his "The Me Decade and the Third Great

Awakening" article in the August 23, 1976, issue of *New York Magazine* the blurb for the article read: "The new alchemical dream is: changing one's personality—remarking, remodeling, elevating, and polishing one's very *self* . . . and observing, studying, doting on it (Me!) . . ."

In a powerful and prescient passage, recounting a moment from a session at Esalen, a communal shrink shop in Big Sur, California, part of something then called the Human Potential Movement, Wolfe wrote: "Each soul is concentrated on its own burning item . . . my husband! my wife! my homosexuality! my inability to communicate, my self-hatred, self-destruction, craven fears, puling weaknesses, primordial horrors, premature ejaculation, impotence, frigidity, rigidity, subservience, laziness, alcoholism, major vices, minor vices, grim habits, twisted psyches, tortured souls—and yet each unique item has been raised to a cosmic level and united with every other" in a feast of self-regard.

A decade earlier than Tom Wolfe's essay, in 1966, the social scientist Philip Rieff published a book with the title *Triumph of the Therapeutic*. In the book Rieff offered a theory of culture that is an impressively persuasive explanation for the rise and triumph of what one thinks of as therapeutic culture. In Rieff's theory, every reigning culture has its interdictory and remissive aspects: The interdicts set out prohibitions, the remissions allow for violating those interdicts. The perfect example, some would say the genius, of Catholic culture is the remissive institution of the confessional allowing release from the Church's strong interdicts

Rieff's theory is itself a theory of history itself, for the argument could be made that history is a continuing, and continuous, chain of changing culture, with sometimes the interdictory becoming too oppressive (as under Soviet Communism), sometimes the remissive, by becoming too antinomian, failing to hold the culture together. "A cultural revolution occurs," Rieff writes, "when the releasing or remissive symbolic grows more compelling than the controlling one; then it is that the inherent tensions reach a breaking point . . ." Too much freedom, Rieff's theory holds, the condition in which the remissive, or freedoms, not only contradicts but works against the interdictory, puts the culture in jeopardy. "Such freedoms," Rieff writes, "were the signatures on the death warrant of previous culture."

These cultural changes, unlike revolutions and coups d'états, occur slowly, almost unnoticeably. Rieff holds that ours, the current therapeutic culture, "is the first cultural revolution fought for no other purpose than greater amplitude and richness of living itself."

The radicalness of the therapeutic revolution lies in more than a simple break with the past moral order but in the attempt to end moral passion itself. Consider the drastically lowered status of sin. "Even now," Rieff writes, "sin is all but incomprehensible to [modern men and women] inasmuch as the moral demand system no longer generates powerful feelings of guilt when those inclinations are over-ridden by others for which sin is the ancient name." Besides, as is oft advertised, the assuaging of guilt is one of the things psychotherapy devotes itself to most sedulously.

How did it come about that the therapeutic has seemed to come to reign above all other idea systems? Other historical forces helped bring this about. The arrival of prosperity, which brought the end of scarcity in advanced societies, made many of the old interdictions lose their force. Former elites—political leaders, clergymen—lost their authority, and no other group has come to the fore. Communism went under; socialism lost its vigor both as an economic system and as a system of belief. The therapeutic became the model, with even Jesus Christ emerging, in some views, as the ultimate therapist. Everywhere everyone holds self-fulfillment as the first order of business; self-esteem is a *sine qua non* for decent living. "That a sense of well-being has become the end, rather than a by-product of striving after some communal end," Rieff writes in the closing sentence of his book, "announces a fundamental shift of focus in the entire cast of our culture . . ."

This shift has come about even though the thought of most of the principal theorists of the therapeutic have by now been disqualified. By which I mean the central ideas of Freud, Jung, and other psychological thinkers are no longer taken seriously by serious people. Those who continue to believe in Sigmund Freud's Oedipus Complex—"Greek myths covering private parts," Vladimir Nabokov called Freudianism—or in the efficacy of psychoanalysis in bringing about cure are surely a vast minority. Jung's belief in the collective unconscious is by no means shared, collectively or otherwise. Karen Horney's view that breast-feeding was absolutely crucial to full human development may be said, in the argot of the young, to suck. As for Wilhelm Reich's orgone box, once believed in by such intellectual figures as Saul Bellow and Isaac Rosenfeld and others, it now seems pure comedy, material for a good bit by Mel Brooks or Larry David. Yet despite this, the defeat of its discrete ideas, the therapeutic as a mode of thought, as a reigning spirit, has nevertheless prevailed and pervades the social and intellectual atmosphere.

What remains of the great age of psychotherapists is no one idea or even series of ideas, but instead such general notions that hold an active sex life (apart from procreation) is central, indeed essential, to the good life, that confession brought about by easy intimacy is healthy and everywhere to be not merely tolerated but encouraged, and above all repression, the arch-enemy, is to be avoided. One sees these notions played out everywhere. In contemporary life what is taken to be psychological health ranks well above moral scrupulosity. The individual thought of Freud, Jung, Reich & Co. may seem to have been defeated idea by idea, yet as of the moment victory is nonetheless theirs.

The result is that the psychotherapeutic has swept the boards, won the day, exercising a subtle but genuine tyranny throughout contemporary culture. Therapy, as Philip Rieff had it, has indeed been triumphant. Anyone older than seventy will recall a time when people were what I think of as "pre-psychological," with morality and stern common sense in command. I think of my own parents here. If I had said to my father that I felt "insecure" about something, he, a gentle and good man, would have told me to pull up my socks and not be a coward. When my mother turned eighty, she was discovered to have liver cancer. Enrolled in a chemotherapy regimen, she nevertheless was fairly (and rightly) certain of her death, which left her, with good reason, mildly depressed. I mentioned her depression to an acquaintance, who told me that there were many support groups for people with terminal illnesses, and perhaps one of them might be helpful for my mother. I imagined her response to my telling her this.

"Let me understand," I can easily hear my mother saying. "You're saying that if I go into a room with strangers and listen to their problems and then tell them mine that I shall feel better for doing so. Is that what you are suggesting? [Pause.] Is this the kind of idiot I have for a son?"

To the extent that the therapeutic has triumphed, charm has been defeated. Not that therapy is itself evil or vile, though it is surely too frequently called into play and too often misbegotten and can be tyrannical. Insofar as it is interested in cure, psychotherapy is another of the healing arts, like orthopedics, cardiology, urology, dermatology, and the rest. The difference is that these latter branches of medicine, unlike the psychotherapeutic, do not go beyond anatomy and physiology to posit a preferred way of living. Other branches of medicine are concerned with healthy organs and bones. Psychotherapy, like most religions, sets out to teach its patients how to live; it offers a model of the good life. This life, featuring devotion to one's own well-being, is implicitly understood to be superior to all other modes of life that have come before it.

The triumph of the therapeutic would never have resulted if other, older cultural systems didn't seem to have broken down. "At the breaking point," Philip Rieff writes in his final chapter, "a culture can no longer maintain itself as an established span of moral demands. Its jurisdiction contracts; it demands less, permits more. Bread and circuses become confused with right and duty." The mention of bread and circuses of course calls up Rome, where luxury and hedonism generally broke down the Roman military and communal spirit, with Christianity, a much more forgiving culture, picking up the pieces and eventually conquering. Might it be that now even Christianity, despite its strong doctrine of forgiveness, is too forbidding for the modern temper?

A cultural revolution is never so clearly marked an event as a political revolution. We think of 1776, 1789, 1917—but there are no precise dates for cultural revolutions, which nevertheless occur and usually establish themselves with greater pervasiveness and efficacy than political ones. Among cultural revolutions, Rieff held that the therapeutic revolution "cannot be viewed simply as a break with the established order of moral demand, but rather as a profound effort to end the tyranny of primary group moral passion . . . as the inner dynamic of the moral order." So widespread has been the cultural victory of the therapeutic, that even once reticent movie action heroes are given to confession, weeping, open displays of sadness. In a book titled *The Origins of the Cool in Postwar America,* Joel Dinerstein, after recounting the reticent style of such film noir heroes as Humphrey Bogart, Alan Ladd, and Robert Mitchum, notes that in the movies of Marlon Brando, James Dean, and others "neurosis was no longer suppressed but expressed, a sign of how deeply psychoanalysis had penetrated artistic and intellectual communities." Dinerstein goes on to refer to Brando as showing the "liberatory energies of the therapeutic man." As Stanley Kowalski, his signature role in *Streetcar Named Desire,* Brando cries in remorse for his treatment of his wife. Difficult to imagine Bogart in any of his roles crying, but then Bogart's movies were made before the triumph of the therapeutic.

If Marlon Brando in his movie roles is therapeutic man, surely therapeutic woman is Oprah Winfrey. Her career seems to have broken through on a confessional note of her own: that of her chronicling, on television, the sexual abuse she suffered as a child. Her battle against weight gain has been a saga now running into the decades. A splendid interview for her was one in which she gets a guest to open herself up before the vast numbers who used to watch her show and reveal her weakness, sadness, fears, wretched past, and anything else that happens to be on hand. The enormous success of Oprah Winfrey, who neither sings nor dances nor is especially penetrating in her conversation, would not have been thinkable in any other than a therapeutic age.

The larger point is that the therapeutic is personal, individual, while charm operates under the aegis of the social, the communal. To confess, though it might conduce to greater intimacy, is never charming; not to repress—"The enemy is repression," said one of the producers of the movie *La La Land,* holding up his Oscar for the year's best film (2017) before it was taken away from him owing to a mistake—might make for psychic health but also for hellish social relations. One of the first rules for charm, surely, is not to say precisely what one thinks and certainly not as soon as one thinks it.

The therapeutic culture is devoted to the self. In the root sense, it is selfish. The charming person asks, "How may I please?"; the therapeutic patient or person asks, "How do I please myself?" The charming person looks outward; the therapeutic person inward. The charming person is never touchy; the therapeutic patient tends to be edgy, on the qui vive for innuendo, insult, hidden aggressions. The first person I ever encountered in therapy was the young husband of a sister of a boyhood friend of mine, who was undergoing a training analysis for his own future career as a psychoanalyst. "Be careful around Dover," my friend told me, "he's in the middle of his training analysis."

The charming person is always tactful—tactful and tasteful. The therapeutic person, setting tact and taste aside, is primarily interested in psychic health; no subject is out of bounds that touches upon or might affect it. In Chicago there has for some years now been a sex-advice columnist who writes a column for a giveaway paper called *The Reader*. He dispenses advice on efficient sodomy, the varied and intricate uses of the clitoris, the ranges of sadomasochism, including stoppage of breath by choking during fornication. He advises his readers to be adventurous. "I'm not saying you have to be nonmonogamous," he writes. "I'm saying a couple can be exclusive and sexually adventurous at the same time." People write to him under stage or therapy names. "Trembling Man" writes to him about his panty-wearing fetish, to which our columnist responds: "There are women out there who think men can be sexy in panties—and anyone who thinks men can't be sexy in panties needs to check out all the hunky panty wearing models at xdress.com." *Charmant?* You decide.

Owing to the triumph of the therapeutic, actors in our day feel perfectly comfortable going on talk shows, or writing full-blown books, discussing their mistreatment by sexually perverse fathers, alcoholic mothers, brutish husbands. Others go on television to speak of their "sex addiction"—as if every healthy man between the ages of fifteen and thirty-five isn't addicted to sex—and their attempts to defeat it. Actresses recount their battles with drugs. Why not? Why hold back? Repression is the enemy, confession good, if not for the soul, certainly for the psyche.

In contemporary writing, the sobbing memoir has become common currency, the genre of the day. Novelists, poets, critics, journalists learn that they are to die and see in it a promising subject for a book, or novel, or poems: Christopher Hitchens, Jenny Diski, Clive James have all played the literary death game, writing about their imminent death in public. Others must be content with exposing their parents or former husbands and wives, noting the heavy mental torture they had visited upon them.

Widened tolerance for irregular behavior, which the age of the thera-peutic has brought, has been offset by the diminishment of decorum that is part of the therapeutic bargain. Vast is the pain that the psychotherapy, greatly aided in recent decades by pharmacology, has relieved, from that of raving paranoid schizophrenics to those born with genetic mis-wiring to those depressed and otherwise defeated by misfortune in life. Much can be said about the use and value of psychotherapy, but its toll on charm has been heavy.

Chapter XIV

Charmless Politics

THE REASON SALESMEN, BARBERS, AND OTHERS DEALING WITH THE GENERAL public are instructed to avoid the topics of religion and politics is that these are the two general subjects that most readily inflame people and are most likely quickly to get the conversation to the shouting stage. The reason religion is an outlawed subject is obvious; it is in the realm of the sacred, and therefore not a fit subject either for trivial conversation or one finally open to argument without touching on the deepest and most tender feelings. As for politics, Jonathan Swift said that one cannot reason people out of something they haven't been reasoned into, and over the years there has been less and less evidence to prove that politics, at least people's personal politics, has all that much to do with reason.

Politics aren't about politics merely—about how people should be governed, about the proper distribution of power and wealth, about just social arrangements—but about something much more personal. More and more in our time politics are expressions, in one form or another, of personal virtue. Disagree with my politics and you are telling me that I am not a good person—certainly not as good as you. Which figures to tick me, as I've no doubt it would tick you, to the max. Whenever I sense people want to argue politics with me—which, I'm pleased to report, isn't very often—I warn them that they ought to know beforehand that I have never lost a political argument, a fact whose impressiveness is offset only by the countervailing fact that neither have I ever won one. The reason is that, *pace* Jonathan Swift, we do not come into our politics through reason and so thereby cannot expect to be argued out of them, or argue anyone else out of theirs, by reason.

Some of us adopt the politics we do because they were the politics of our parents; others because they are strongly opposed to those of our parents. One's milieu—be it the corporation, the university, the country club, or the neighborhood bar—can be decisive in forming one's politics. Over and above all this there are the competing virtues that lie behind politics, entailing such issues, or points in contention, as abortion, climate change, the distribution of income, and the rest. The liberal or progressive finds his virtue in what he thinks a strong sense of social justice, the conservative his in an equally strong sense of the importance of liberty for the formation of character. The liberal thinks the conservative hard-hearted, the conservative thinks the liberal hopelessly naïve about human nature. Liberal and conservative, each faces the other confident of the superiority of his or her intelligence and virtue over that of the other.

Besides, there is something coarsening about the certainty of views held by intensely political people—a certainty and aggressiveness that works against the nature of charm. H. L. Mencken, in *Minority Report,* captured this quality neatly when he wrote:

> *Moral certainty is always a sign of cultural inferiority. The more uncivi-*
> *lized the man, the surer he is that he knows precisely what is right and*
> *what is wrong. All human progress, even in morals, has been the work of*
> *men who have doubted the current moral values, not of men who have*
> *whooped them up and tried to enforce them. The truly civilized man is*
> *always skeptical and tolerant, in this field as in all others. His culture is*
> *based on "I am not too sure."*

Because of its inherent contentiousness, politics has never been an arena in which charm has flourished. To be sure, politicians are often called upon to charm supporters, colleagues, voters. A politician utterly bereft of charm, unless he be a ruthless dictator—a Nero, a Hitler, a Stalin—would be in difficult straits, certainly in electoral politics. But his charm is likely to have its limits, and these figure to be strict. Franklin Delano Roosevelt is said to have been charming. He charmed the coldhearted Walter Winchell, who, through his newspaper columns, rallied support for all Roosevelt's programs. Yet during his years in office, nearly half the country—that ample portion that didn't vote for him, or hold with his general ideas—not merely disliked but greatly loathed him. Some of the nuttier among his haters, thinking to cash in a chip of anti-Semitism while at it, claimed he was Jewish, real name Rosenberg.

When I asked friends and acquaintances to name five charming figures in public life, not a few mentioned Barack Obama, one or two named Michelle Obama. Quite as many people, however, intensely disliked the Obamas, and not for reasons of race. They disliked Barack Obama's policies; his taking sides other than theirs in foreign and domestic policy; they thought Michelle Obama stiff, unconvincing in her avowed sensitivity, ultimately phony and trivial with her campaign against obesity. One measure of an American president's charm, though a vastly inexact one, is his approval rating; and for much of his eight years in office, Barack Obama's hovered under 50 percent. In the current American political atmosphere of intense political disagreement, that may be the best any American president in our day can hope for. Our current president has yet to get anywhere close to a 50 percent approval rating, though, true enough, no one, even among his most ardent supporters would ever think to call him charming to begin with. So much does he bring out the unpleasant passions in people—his defenders and contemners alike—that in a biweekly meeting with old friends I have instituted a no-Trump-talk rule.

If ever one wishes to view a politician at his most charming, one might look into the charm Benjamin Disraeli turned on Queen Victoria. The stern queen and the rather exotic Jew who had climbed what he called "the greasy pole" of politics to rise to its top as Tory prime minister of England would seem the oddest of odd couples. "I live for Power and Affections," Disraeli claimed, and from Victoria, through his charm, he managed to wring both. How he amused the woman known for so frequently uttering "We are not amused" is no great secret. He expressed unstinting admiration for her beloved Albert. By the time of his second prime-ministership (1874–1880), he, Disraeli, joined her in widow(er) hood, which made for a bond of mutual sympathy between them. In her, he found his ambition as a social climber fulfilled beyond all possible expectation. In him, she found a friend, full, as she wrote, of "romance, poetry, and chivalry." He wrote her gossip-filled letters, took care of those little but bedeviling tasks that might otherwise have complicated her life, addressed her, this small, buxom, double-chinned, middle-age woman, as "Faery Queen." And she went for it, hook, line, and sceptre. Lytton Strachey, in his appreciative biography, *Queen Victoria*, writes:

> He [Disraeli] had understood from the first that in dealing with the Faery the appropriate method of approach . . . It was not his habit to harangue and exhort and expatiate in official conscientiousness; he liked to scatter flowers along the path of business, to compress a weighty argument into a happy phrase, to insinuate what was in his mind with an air of friendship and confidential courtesy. He was nothing if not personal; and he had perceived that personality was the key to the Faery's heart. Accordingly, he never for a moment allowed his intercourse with her to lose the personal tone; he invested all the transactions of State with the charms of familiar conversation; she was always the royal, the adored and revered mistress, he the devoted and respectful friend. When once the personal relation was firmly established, every difficulty disappeared . . .
>
> She became intoxicated, entranced. Believing all he told her about herself, she completely regained the self-confidence which had been slipping away from her throughout the dark period that followed Albert's death. She swelled with a new elation, while he, conjuring up before her wonderful Oriental visions, dazzled her eyes with imperial grandeur of which she had only dimly dreamed. Under the compelling influence, her very demeanour altered. Her short, stout figure, with its folds of black velvet, its muslin streamers, its heavy pearls at the heavy neck, assumed an almost menacing air. In her countenance, from which the charm of youth had long since vanished, and which had not yet been softened by age, the traces of grief, of disappointment, and of displeasure were still visible, but they were overlaid by looks of arrogance and sharp lines of peremptory hauteur. Only, when Mr. Disraeli appeared, the expression changed in an instant, and the forbidding visage became charged with smiles.

Although thought a popular politician, popular in spite of his Jewishness in an overwhelmingly Christian country, Disraeli was removed from office in 1880 in an election that saw his conservative party trounced. Which goes to show that in politics charm may take a person quite far, but it won't keep him in office.

Winston Churchill, easily the most decisive British, if not Western, political figure in the twentieth century, was never short on charm. Endless are the amusing quotations attributed to him, most got off at sumptuous dinner parties at which he supplied not only the fare but the wit. "I have in my life," he said, "concentrated more on self-expression than on self-denial." He declared himself "a man of simple tastes—I am quite easily satisfied with the best of everything." His amusing sayings on booze alone would fill a handsome chapbook. "I could not live without champagne," he said. "In victory I deserve it. In defeat I need it." And: "When I was younger I made it a rule never to take strong drink before lunch. It is now my rule never to do so before breakfast." He wasn't bad at repartee either. Nancy Astor told him that if she were married to him she would put poison in his coffee, to which he retorted, "If I were married to you, I'd drink it." On more worldly matters he announced that "there are a terrible lot of lies going round the world, and the worst of it is that half of them are true." He held that "we are all worms. But I do believe that I am a glow worm."

Glow with charm Churchill did, triumphantly, steadfastly through a long career with many up and downs. His greatest triumph, for which the world owes him an unpayable debt, was the steadfastness he showed in holding the line and leading his country against the hideous depredations of Adolf Hitler, and thereby contributing as much as any single figure to saving the West from the thousand-year nightmare of the Third Reich. In gratitude, such is politics, despite the courage or charm of this greatest of politicians, Winston Churchill's countrymen voted him out of power in 1945 shortly after the end of World War Two.

No American politicians demonstrated charm comparable to Disraeli or Churchill's. Perhaps the most charming American politician in the post–World War Two era, Adlai Stevenson, was twice defeated for the presidency. John F. Kennedy was thought charming, yet he seems to have said nothing notable that wasn't written for him. Apart from those utterly bewitched by the Kennedy myth, his sexual predatoriness—described earlier—detracts greatly from his reputation for charm. His father's ugly social views—an anti-Semite, a friend to Hitler's Germany—he, the son, never properly repudiated. John F. Kennedy's putative charm in the end seems less real than a product of his administration's brilliant public relations effort—Camelot and all that—and not something in which the discerning believe.

In his public persona Lyndon Johnson seemed the very reverse of charming—stiff and false ("Muh fella Amuricans . . ."). The reason may well have been that the real Lyndon Johnson was too raw for public consumption. This is the Lyndon Johnson who one evening during his presidency, at a cocktail party, pointed to his vice president, Hubert Humphrey, across the room, and remarked, "See that old boy? I've got his pecker in my pocket"; referred to his wife as "best piece I've ever had"; and called C. Douglas Dillon, his Secretary of the Treasury, into the bathroom to discuss monetary policy while he, LBJ, sat there defecating. Possibly amusing, if one has a taste for humiliating one's employees, but a long way from charming, though some might wish to argue that Johnson qualifies as one of my vulgar charmers.

Many people, the journalist Tina Brown among others, spoke of the charm of Bill Clinton—she remarked of the tremendous radiance he gave off upon meeting him—but this was before the Monica Lewinsky scandal that quickly let the air out of that good old boy's charm. Charm does not reside easily beside squalor.

No one ever called either of the Bushes, *père ou fils*, charming, though I was once, for all of thirty minutes, in the oval office of the White House, where I heard a woman named Edith Kurzweil, an émigré from Germany, upon receiving an award, say to George W. Bush, "I never believed I would be in this room," to which he replied, "Neither did I." Forgive me if I confess to finding that charming.

The charm, or even memorably charming moments, of a small number of politicians is one thing, the loss of charm by otherwise possibly charming people by taking up political positions is quite another. Movie stars, athletes, singers have had their politics, but the wiser among them chose to keep them to themselves. The career of San Francisco 49ers' quarterback Colin Kaepernick went down the tubes when for political reasons he refused to stand for the playing of "The Star Spangled Banner" before games. Most people prefer their athletes to remain on the field and out of the political arena.

Hollywood has always been political. In the 1930s and '40s it was said that Stalinists in Hollywood were far from a minority, even though the great studio bosses were extremely nervous about tipping their own political mitts or allowing politics to intrude in their movies lest they adversely affect the box office. These same studio bosses—Louis B. Mayer, Samuel Goldwyn, David O. Selznick, and others—were able to keep the lid tightly down on their actors' political views, or at least on their not allowing them to be known. But politics, being as natural to men and women as appetite, were not everywhere publicly repressed. Hollywood was roughly divided between liberals and conservatives. Frank Sinatra was in earlier days in the liberal camp, and so was Gene Kelly, whose wife Betsy Drake was thought to be a fellow traveler if not a member of the American Communist Party. (During the House on UnAmerican Affairs Committee hearings, Kelly and his wife felt the need to leave the country for Europe for a few years, lest her politics be exposed, a move that is said to have slowed her husband's career.) On the other side, James Stewart was a stalwart conservative; Fred Astaire, who kept his politics to himself, voted Republican; and during the Vietnam War John Wayne carried a Zippo lighter on which were engraved the words "Fuck Communism." But all this, on both sides, was sub-rosa, literally hidden under the roses, figuratively meaning not on any account to be revealed.

The ban on political expression for movie stars ended with the simultaneous student protest movement against the Vietnam War and the end of the studio system in Hollywood. With no studio executives bearing down on them, actors could declare their political views openly. Some thought this brave; others thought bravery had little to do with it, and in doing so they were instead engaging in what today is called virtue-signalling, which is to say, displaying their own goodness in public.

From Marlon Brando's boycotting the Oscars in protest of the treatment of American Indians in movies to Meryl Streep's upbraiding Donald

Trump for mocking a handicapped journalist, Hollywood actors have, so to say, tried on the role of moral leaders. The role calls for what they are doing to seem both passionate and brave. Since the political culture of Hollywood has been preponderantly progressive for decades now, an actor publicly announcing him- or herself in favor of a liberal cause or opposed to a conservative politician is, however true his or her feeling for the cause, essentially joining the herd of independent minds. As for bravery in the realm of political opinion, I am reminded that many years ago my friend, the social scientist Edward Shils, after giving a government-sponsored Jefferson Lecture about the coarsening effect of the federal government on academic life, was greeted at the lectern by an admirer, who told him how brave he thought his lecture was. "Thank you," Edward said, "but it wasn't in the least brave. Brave is living in South Africa and speaking out against apartheid, brave is publishing dissenting works in the Soviet Union. Brave is when there is a severe penalty likely to follow from your actions. Far from this being the case with my lecture, I was paid a $10,000 fee for it by the same federal government I attacked."

In the public realm one cannot charm some of the people some of the time. To qualify as charming one must charm most of the people most of the time. Charm requires consensus. When a public figure declares his politics, along with losing a large portion of his audience, he gives up any hope of establishing that consensus about his own charm. The divisive field of politics is the last place for charmers to work their magic. That the current age happens to be as politically divisive as any on recent record is one of the principal reasons charm is itself onto lean times in our day. Athlete, movie star, actor, singer, private person, if any among them wish to establish themselves as charming, all do best to steer well clear of politics.

CHAPTER XV

The New Shabby Chic

IN A LOOSE USE OF THE WORD, A YOUNG CHILD MIGHT BE CALLED CHARMING, so, too a kitten, or a doll. In these instances not *charming* but *cute* would likely be the more precise word. Inanimate objects can be charming: a painting, a poem, or an eighteenth-century clock; so, too, can an artistic creation, a poem, a building, a song be charming. But charm as the power to delight, elevate, and render the world a place full of possibilities is restricted to human beings, and all but exclusively to adults of the species. Charm is an adult phenomenon, skill, art. Charm is worldly, a quality available only to those who have a considerable and considered experience of the wider world.

In an essay in the *Atlantic* (June 2013), Benjamin Schwarz writes:

[Charm] simultaneously demands detachment and engagement. Only the self-aware can have charm: it's bound up with a sensibility that at best approaches wisdom, or at least worldliness, and at worst goes well beyond cynicism. It can't exist in the undeveloped personality. It's an attribute foreign to many men because most are, for better or worse, child-like. These days, it's far more common among men over 70—probably owing to the era in which they reached maturity rather than to the mere fact of their advanced years.

In other words, to be charming one has to be adult, and to be fully adult one might just have to have grown up before the cultural reign of the 1960s set in.

Among the enemies of charm thus far considered—psychotherapy for encouraging confession and discouraging useful repression and thoughtful reticence, politics for its inherent divisiveness—must be added the closing down of adulthood, a phenomenon that has been on the move in the United States and much of Europe since the 1960s. The notion of "the closing down of adulthood" might strike some as hyperbole. I don't believe it hyperbolic in the least; I believe that adulthood is no longer an admired condition or state; I believe that for most people the longer it can be put off, including nearly forever, the better. Most people, males especially, would seem to prefer to live a life of perpetual adolescence.

As for how this came about, one might begin with the discovery in the late 1950s and early 1960s on the part of advertising agencies and retailers of the emergence of the young—specifically of teenagers—as a separate and profitable market for goods and entertainment. Suddenly the young were catered to in a way they never quite were before: Social arrangements changed to make way for them, special clothes were made for them, television shows devised with them in mind, music composed and recorded for them alone. Before the discovery of youth as a specifically marketed target, the United States had a unified culture in which three generations of a family might sit before the television set to watch the same shows—*Ed Sullivan's Toast of the Town*, say, or *The Carol Burnett Show*—afterward the country was divided between the young and the not young.

The reverence for youth or the young, even for the prenatal, is not an entirely new phenomenon. Plato thought we were at our wisest when still in the womb. Wordsworth, in his poem "Intimations of Immortality," held that we are born with great wisdom that life through the agency of a corrupting society causes us to forget. In writing about the Jazz Age, the period between the end of World War One and the beginning of the Depression, F. Scott Fitzgerald remarked upon the older generation catching up with the younger. In his essay, "Echoes of the Jazz Age," he wrote:

> *Scarcely had the staider citizens of the republic caught their breaths, when the wildest of all generations, the generation which had been adolescent during the confusion of the War, brusquely shouldered my contemporaries out of the way and danced into the limelight. This was the generation*

*whose girls dramatized themselves as flappers, the generation that cor-
rupted its elders and eventually overreached itself less through lack of morals than through lack of taste . . . The sequel was rather like a children's
party taken over by the elders, leaving the children puzzled and rather
neglected and rather taken aback.*

In 1960, John F. Kennedy was elected president of the United States.
The upsurge in youth adoration perhaps begins here, with the young Jack
Kennedy, leader of the world's most powerful country who does not wear
an adult hat and is often photographed playing touch football or sailing.
(He also golfed, but the press agreed not to photograph him doing so, for
President Eisenhower's golfing, considered a great time-waster, had gotten
bad press.) The accent in the Kennedy administration on youthfulness
initiated the new hunger to stay young.

In the middle 1960s, the age known with chronological inexactitude
as the Sixties, the student protest movement, kicked in. "The establishment" was the name given to the enemies of the students in their protests,
but the real enemies were their elders, if not adulthood generally. "Never
trust anyone over thirty" was one of the movement's leading shibboleths.
What was really meant was never trust anyone who seems staid, respectable, middle-class—in short, never trust grown-ups.

Although the student protest movement eventually subsided and
seemed to have disappeared, it was perhaps more victorious, in the cultural
than the political realm, than its many followers and enemies know. As I
mentioned earlier, cultural revolution is always more efficacious than political revolution. Before long people over thirty themselves no longer trusted
anyone over thirty. In fifteen or twenty years many of the students who
led or signed up for the protests were themselves professors in the same
universities they once found so oppressive, and not long after their youthful
views began to prevail through their teaching of oncoming generations.

One could tell the academic troops from the 1960s by the way they
dressed (jean-clad and bearded), spoke to students (without formality,
even intimately), and taught their subjects (with an eye to the reform
and ultimate enlightenment of humankind, at least as they construed
enlightenment, by emphasizing the centrality of race, class, and gender in

humanistic and social scientific studies). Soon enough the Zeitgeist, the time-spirit, had changed, decisively, in favor of youthfulness, no matter how old its old advocates grew.

The Sixties generation eschewed elegance for naturalness. The notion of ugliness was replaced by oldliness as the repulsive condition. "It grows harder to write," noted F. Scott Fitzgerald many decades before, "because there is much less weather than when I was a boy, and practically no men and women at all." The loss of an adult population that Fitzgerald bemoaned has since thinned out much further, well beyond his by-no-means imperceptive imagining.

Youth was once understood to be a transient state through which one passed after childhood and on the way to adulthood. Then, in the middle and late 1960s, it became a social class—and an aggrieved and angry one, whose enemies were its elders but also the middle class and its way of life at large. Then, when the tumult of the 1960s died down—Vietnam ignominiously ended, student and graduate-student days done—the need to get into the main flow of life beckoning, youth became neither a transient state nor a social class but a desideratum, a goal, an ideal. Two of the greatest compliments in America in our day are: "You look thin" and "You don't at all look your age." "Grow up," wrote Fitzgerald, anticipating our own time, "that is a terribly hard thing to do. It is much easier to skip it and go from one childhood to another." And that, in many respects, is what our contemporary culture appears not merely to have encouraged but to have done.

Nature of course has other ideas. As one advances through life it wrinkles the skin, grays or removes the hair, alters posture, hands out funny walks and imperishable blemishes, diminishes pleasurable appetites. To combat these depredations there are cosmetic surgery, hair dyes ("He paints his head," said the Romans in derision of those who wished to hide their gray hair), wigs, gymnasiums and personal trainers and spas, erection-inducing pills. Juan Ponce de Leon thou shouldst be alive at this hour.

Yet, if Ponce de Leon were alive now, viewing older billionaires with oxblood-colored hair, aging actresses with skin made so tight by cosmetic surgery they cannot close their eyes at night, old men whose jogging pace resembles infants just beginning to walk, former 1960s student radicals sporting sad gray ponytails or topknots, perhaps the Spanish explorer would have given up his (legendary) search for the Fountain of Youth, and resigned himself to aging as gracefully as possible. "Obviously," wrote W. H. Auden, himself a youngest son, "it is normal to think oneself younger than one is, but fatal to want to be younger."

Not merely the people who can afford to get "work" done, as cosmetic surgery is euphemistically denoted, or those dedicated to the rigors of the gym when their bodies are long beyond help, are afflicted with what I think of as the youth virus. Something more in the nature of a pandemic is entailed, and it is the triumph of the youth culture over an entire society. Earlier in this book I mentioned asking friends and acquaintances to name five people in public life who are charming. An only slightly less difficult question today might be to ask them to name five people who are adults.

Think of the current crop of aging movie stars. Robert Redford, for example, though now in his eighties, goes about bejeaned, dressed as a boy, with deeply tanned yet wrinkled skin and dyed hair. Jim Carrey, whose career has faded, played chiefly comic-book characters in his movies, and now in his middle fifties seems himself a comic-book character. Women movie stars are not allowed to age, and so, with a few notable exceptions—Meryl Streep chief among them—they simply fade away. No graceful closing down of careers, such as was allowed Katherine Hepburn and Barbara Stanwyck and Bette Davis, is permitted. Youth may be, as Shaw had it, wasted on the young, but perhaps it's not wasted after all if one refuses to grow older.

Two of the most successful sitcoms of recent decades, *Seinfeld* and *Friends*, were about the refusal of their characters to grow up. Both were very amusing—*Seinfeld* was the last television sitcom I looked forward to watching—but none of them contained characters in the least charming. Quite the reverse. *Seinfeld*'s continuing theme was the selfishness of people refusing to grow up—a theme that, in its egregiousness, was of course played for laughs. No one on *Friends* had a serious job, or seemed likely to get one soon. The characters on both shows were somewhere roughly between their late twenties and mid-thirties. Adulthood for any of them was nowhere in sight.

Nor apparently is it in sight for many of the aging young today. Although I have tried not to include so-called "studies" in this book, I cannot resist quoting a recent Pew Research study that found that "for the first time in more than 130 years adults age 18 to 34 were slightly more than likely to be living in their parents' home than they were living with a spouse or partner in their own home." Something on the order of a quarter of all Americans between the ages of twenty-five and twenty-nine lived with parents. One could, I suppose, blame this on the sluggish economy, but I strongly suspect the blame is owing to the culture of youth, which holds that one really needn't consider oneself on one's own till well past thirty. As the Jerry Seinfeld character on *Seinfeld* might say, "Not that there is anything wrong with it." Except of course that, given the wasted years of possible accomplishment in life, there is.

Tom Wolfe has remarked that the current stages of growth in America are from juvenility to senility, with no stops in between. One sees one of the victories of the youth culture in the clothes people wear, myself included. As I tap away at these sentences I am wearing chino pants, a white polo shirt under a blue V-neck sweater, and penny loafers—an outfit closely resembling those I went off in to Nicholas Senn High School in Chicago sixty-three and more years ago. I think here of my mother, who never left the house without full makeup, an elegant dress, heels. Or of my father, who until the last years of his life, had no clothes for leisure—only business suits—and never left the house without his fedora and shined shoes. "No one except lawyers buy suits anymore," a haberdasher of my acquaintance told me a few years ago. "Lawyers still buy them, but only because they need them for courtroom appearances and to impress clients with their ostensible seriousness."

Before the 1960s, California, with its spirit of informality, had a fair amount to do with loosening up the standard adult dress code. Suits and ties for men, dresses and heels for women, were replaced by open collars, slacks, shorts, and sandals. But more than a loosening up has taken place since. For decades now, putative grown-ups have been dressing down, as in dumbing down. This is commonplace in universities, where professors with distinguished titles after their names—the Benjamin and Bessie Nurishkeit Professor of Sociology—walk into classes tieless, wearing baseball caps (some worn backward), shod in Air Jordans, toting backpacks. And not in universities alone. (One of my favorite scenes from *The Sopranos* has Tony Soprano dining with his family in a restaurant, when he spots a man at another table eating his dinner wearing a baseball cap. Unable to bear what he takes to be the disrespect of someone not bothering to remove a childish hat in a good restaurant, Tony goes up to the man's table and in a quiet but unmistakably menacing voice instructs the man to remove his cap forthwith, which, getting the unmistakable message, he quickly does.) Everywhere one sees men and women in their fifties, sixties, seventies, eighties in what I think of as one form or another of youth drag.

A standard youth drag outfit for men features a baseball cap, gym shoes, shirt worn untucked into pants, usually jeans. (When the definitive history of the decline of the West comes to be written, a substantial chapter will be devoted to jeans.) For women, who on balance seem to go in for youth drag in lesser numbers than do men, jeans and baseball caps may also be part of the getup; black tights currently often replace jeans, without regard for the absence of the svelte figure that such tights require. Older men wear cargo shorts in warm weather; women who no longer have the skin for it don tank tops. Along with this dressing down, a high degree of simple schlepperosity has set in. I see older men, unshaven, in shorts, shirt out, baseball cap atop their gray heads, out on the street in a state that fifty or so years ago their fathers wouldn't have worn to take out the garbage, lest neighbors see them in such a state of deshabille. "It does not become a man of years," said Goethe, no dope, "to follow the fashion either in ideas or dress."

This new schlepperosity is apparently not a purely American phenomenon. In an article in the London *Daily Mail* about the English playwright Tom Stoppard's eightieth birthday party, photographs of famous English actors who attended the party show a similar deshabille look. There is Michael Gambon, who seems to have forgotten to brush his hair; Iain Glen in flip-flops; Sir Tim Rice in jeans; Damien Leigh with his shirt untucked and a handkerchief sticking out of his pocket; Jeremy Irons in an unpressed suit and red sneakers; Michael Kitchen with his shirt not quite tucked in and hair not quite combed; Jude Law in a wife-beater undershirt exposed under an unbuttoned shirt; and the birthday celebrant himself unkempt and wearing an emphatically rumpled chambray work shirt. Are we at the presence here of a new mode of dress, let us call it "shabby-chic," the unmade-bed look.

Capitalism, clever dog, is rarely thrown by revolution, and never by changes in social mores. The new styles in clothing are available for the rich and famous in designer labels at top prices. Prada sells prewashed jeans for $365, Yves Saint-Laurent offers a chambray work shirt for $900, fake fatigue jackets go for as much as $1,000. Only under capitalism can one dress badly but still expensively.

In my own neighborhood, the middle-to-upper-middle-class one of downtown Evanston, Illinois, no one who looks distinctive, let alone distinguished, seems to pass on the thoroughfare before our apartment building for days at a time. A dreary sameness of the relentlessly casual is on parade: backpacks, baseball caps, jeans, gym shoes, worn by people of all ages, college students and habitués of retirement homes alike. The old innovation of Casual Friday has been turned into Casual Every Day. Viewing the parade of contemporary humanity, the word *drab* comes to mind, and stays there. So drab is the apparel worn by the people who pass through the neighborhood that the other day two young women, Chinese, doubtless students at nearby Northwestern University, passed the busy corner across from my building on their way perhaps to a party, possibly a wedding. They had artfully applied makeup. They were in modestly high heels. One had on a dress of blue chiffon, the other was in black. They dazzled, not just me, but, it was plain, all those who passed them on the street. Amid the others walking by in the dull standard getups of the day, they shone with a glamour akin to that of movie stars.

Men, as I say, seem worse offenders than women in the realm of dreary dress, although often, viewed from my sixth-floor apartment, true enough, I cannot tell the difference between men and women from their clothes. Here the popularity of the hooded sweatshirt—the hoodie—comes into play. Nobody's looks are improved by a hoodie. The same holds for beards, scruffy or carefully cut. I know no way of more quickly adding a decade to one's appearance than by the growth of a white beard. "All beards grown after my father's generation are fake," said the great choreographer George Balanchine (1904–1983).

But perhaps the most serious male error of all is the perpetual three- or four-day growth-of-beard, known as double-stubble or permastubble. The provenance of this error is a now-forgotten actor named Don Johnson, who played the leading role with permastubble on a 1980s television show called *Miami Vice*. Johnson was extremely handsome, and probably would have looked good wearing only half a mustache and one sideburn. Every other man sporting it, though, would do well to shave his permastubble instanter; it doesn't work; it chiefly makes those who adopt it look scruffy, grubby, unclean.

While on the subject of hair, the current day has turned up more than its share of misbegotten hairdos. Young—and sometimes not so young—women's penchant for day-glow hair dyes is up there near the top. For men, consider the mullet, short in the front and on the sides, long in the back, a sad spin off on the old and regrettably not yet forgotten tomahawk. Or think of the various moussed-up hairdos, or for that matter of mousse itself. Or of what I think of as the Kim Jong-un look, after the haircut of the current dictator of North Korea, shaved on the sides, moussed up topsides. Let us not forget the vogue for wearing shirts outside of pants, so convenient for men with ample front footage as I have heard vast bellies described. About neck and face tattoos, or the aesthetic of the tattoo generally, let us not speak.

The evidence that clothes can unmake the man and woman and strip both of their charm is vividly on display in the movies of the 1970s. Although women in those years made the mistake of wearing wide-shouldered jackets, men beat them out with such hopeless items as leisure suits, Nehru jackets, long pointed shirt collars, bellbottom trousers, over-the-ears hairdos, sideburns that stopped just short of being muttonchops. ("Damn your sideburns!" says a character in a V. S. Naipaul novel.) So egregious were the clothes and hairstyles worn by actors in the 1970s that the clothes alone make nearly unwatchable even the better movies made during a decade rich in good movies. If the clothes of the 1970s were garish, those of today tend to be sadly dingy.

Clothes in themselves are not charming, but they can be distinctive, elegant, even witty. They can also provide a nice backdrop for charm. Cary Grant wore clothes that qualified on all three counts. So, too, did

Fred Astaire. A decade ago I wrote a little book about Fred Astaire, in which, after remarking on how good he looked in all his carefully chosen clothes, I added: "But think of all the outfits it is impossible to imagine him wearing: visualize him in a football uniform, a Nehru jacket, a tank top, Spandex shorts, a Speedo, a baseball cap turned backward, a backpack, a ponytail, jeans stonewashed, relaxed fit, or any other kind. Not possible!" Fred Astaire, in no small measure owing to his wardrobe, achieved the ideal of the classless aristocrat—the aristocracy, that is, of the talented and the charming. A closed club, this aristocracy, and those in youth drag need not apply for membership.

The pianist Arthur Gold is quoted, in Megan Marshall's recent biography of the poet Elizabeth Bishop, on Ms. Bishop's clothes, and how these contributed to her personality. "There was something physically graceful and very elegant about Elizabeth," Gold writes. "She had what I call genius hair (vibrant, very alive hair); a delightful smile, when she was familiar with you; and a very warm, rather sad, half-shy and half-loving air. She was very, very soignée, always going to the hairdresser, always looking terribly neat, extremely put together, and her clothes were very, very thought out. Elizabeth loved clothes," Gold continues. "They weren't distinguished clothes but always suggested a tiny bit of elegance—not American jazzy elegance."

Santayana thought it a great sin, the greatest, to set out to strangle human nature. The attempt to stay perpetually young is, in our day, the most notable and common way of doing so. The same attempt is perhaps also among the most efficient ways to divest oneself of charm. It is also to miss the bitter joke, the withering irony, that the quickest way to grow old is in the hopeless attempt to stay young. How much more graceful to end up resembling the character Gabriel Varden in *Barnaby Rudge,* of whom Dickens wrote:

> *He was past the prime of life, but Father Time is not always a hard parent, and though he tarries for none of his children, often lays his hand lightly upon those who have used him well, making them old men and women inexorably enough, but leaving their hearts and spirits young and in full vigor. With such people the gray head is but the impression of the*

old fellow's hand in giving them his blessing and every wrinkle but a notch in the quiet calendar of a well-spent life.

Clothes may not make the man and woman, as the old adage had it, but being badly dressed figures to detract from what charm men and women might have to begin with. A charming person, if he or she can help it, shouldn't be a schlepper. Consider Audrey Hepburn in low-slung jeans and a tramp-stamp tattoo showing above her bottom; or Cary Grant in prewashed, leisure-cut jeans and a sad gray ponytail. *Bang!*—in both cases their charm disappears. Does this mean that charm is not merely skin-deep but, more superficial still, no deeper than the clothes that cover that skin? Not at all. What it means is that charm is a combination of verbal skills, physical attributes, dress, psychological insight—all these taken together and more, still more.

CHAPTER XVI

Charm—Who Needs It?

AFTER READING MY LAST THREE CHAPTERS ON THE TOLL TAKEN ON CHARM that the psychotherapeutic spirit, divisive politics, and the rise of youth culture with its accompanying schlepperosity of dress, one might conclude that, if one can avoid these substantial potholes in contemporary life, one has a respectable chance of achieving charm. Would that it were so! Charm is more elusive, more complex, perhaps even more mysterious, than mere avoidance of some of its major contemporary pitfalls would suggest.

Charm may also seem of secondary, if not tertiary, importance in the larger scheme of life. After all, few people have it, most people appear to get on quite nicely without it, some may never have been touched by it, and a small number of others wouldn't know it if they did encounter it. Who, really, needs it?

Charm will not feed the hungry, end wars, fight evil, yet I happen to believe that the lives of almost all of us are the better for encountering charm. Charm provides, among other things, a form of necessary relief— relief from the doldrums, the drab everydayness of life. Sydney Smith, whose own charm I have recounted earlier, wrote that "man could direct his ways by plain reason and support his life by tasteless food; but God has given us wit, and flavour, and brightness, and laughter, and perfumes, to enliven the days of man's pilgrimage and to charm his pained steps over the burning marle." If your vocabulary is as limited as mine, you will have to look up the word *marle*. I'll save you the effort, having just done so myself, to discover that *marle* is "unconsolidated sedimentary rock or soil consisting of clay and lime, formerly used typically as fertilizer." What

Sydney Smith was too charming to say straight out, though I am not, is that charm helps us to get over the crap in life, which, as anyone who lived a respectable number of years will know, can at times be abundant.

In his *Notebooks*, the English philosopher Michael Oakeshott posited an ideal character. The form and content of this ideal character, he held, was composed of integrity, the inheritance of civilization known as culture, and charm, the three joined together by piety, which for Oakeshott doubtless meant reverence for life. As for charm, which one might not have thought such a central quality of the ideal character, Oakeshott wrote: "Charm compensates for the lack of everything else: charm that comes from a sincere and generous spirit. Those who ignore charm & fix their appreciation upon what they consider more solid virtues are, in fact, ignoring mortality. Mortality is the rationale of the primacy of charm."

What do you suppose Oakeshott meant by that last sentence: "Mortality is the rationale of the primacy of charm"? Oakeshott himself, in his *Notebooks*, where I discovered the sentence, doesn't elaborate. I believe he meant that, since we all die, are merely mortal, guests here only briefly on Earth, we have an obligation to get the most of our limited time on the planet. Those who ignore charm, then, are ignoring one of life's genuine pleasures, while those who dispense it are adding to the richness of life. So long as we are mortal, charm, in other words, is far from, can never be, negligible.

Some would say that the charming are among the blessed of the world. The English poet and novelist Laurie Lee, in *As I Walked Out One Midsummer Morning*, one of his three autobiographical works, said as much, writing of charm: "It was the ultimate weapon, the supreme seduction . . . If you've got it you need almost nothing else, neither money, nor looks, nor pedigree. It's a gift only to give way . . . an aura, an invisible musk in the air." The simple disinterestedness of charm, its fine motivelessness, is part of its—well, of its charm.

Charm reminds one of life's lovely possibilities. Even if many of these possibilities are not truly available to us—to sing splendidly, to dance divinely, to compete at sports like a god, to dress elegantly, to display wit casually—it is nevertheless reassuring to know that there are men and women in the world who can and have done these things. Reminding us of life's possibilities, charm elevates the spirit. Life holds the rewards of achievement, acquisition, love of family and friends, but without occasional infusions of charm the enterprise is, somehow, flat, less than complete.

If I am correct in my claims that we live in a time where there is a paucity of charm, what is one to do? Those of us who get high on, groove on, one might say are even addicted to charm find ourselves falling back on the charm of the past: on the movies directed by Leo McCarey and Preston Sturges, acted in by Fred Astaire and Ginger Rogers and Cary Grant and Barbara Stanwyck and William Powell and Myrna Loy and Laurel and Hardy. Add the silent films of Charlie Chaplin and Buster Keaton. Toss in the songs of Johnny Mercer, Cole Porter, the Brothers Gershwin, Harold Arlen, and Jerome Kern; the singing of Louis Armstrong, Alberta Hunter, Bing Crosby, Ella Fitzgerald, Blossom Dearie; the saxophone of Lester Young; the clarinet of Artie Shaw; the big bands of Duke Ellington, Benny Goodman, the Brothers Dorsey. The essays of Charles Lamb and Max Beerbohm, the novels of P. G. Wodehouse and Evelyn Waugh, the poems of Philip Larkin and Ogden Nash all provide charm in its literary division. If all this seems rather light fare, that is because it ought to be, for light, in the most approbative sense, is what charm indubitably is.

Then there is always the hope one will meet a person or two who is a carrier of the lovely charm virus, which fortunately is incurable but not, unfortunately, contagious. I have met such people, though not as often as I would like, finding my spirits, my sense of myself, uplifted in their company. One of the chief things charm does, even if we know we cannot emulate it, is make us feel better about ourselves. Being with charming people can make one feel oneself charming, at least tangentially, at least a little. Those dispensing true charm not only light up rooms but lives.

In 1972, when I was thirty-five, I met a man who asked me what I happened to be reading at the time. "A novel by Alison Lurie," I said. "About academic screwing, I take it," he answered. Correct. Later in the evening I mentioned someone I knew who was a political scientist. "With the science," he added, "understood of course as in Christian Science." He was older than I, twenty-seven years older. I'm not sure what he saw in me, but we became friends, good friends.

He taught at the University of Chicago and at Cambridge in England. He was cosmopolitan, and had spent a good deal of time in past years in

India, Holland, Germany. He savored nationality traits. I once had lunch with him and a famous historian of the French Revolution. After lunch, he asked me what I thought of the historian. "A very nice man, but there was something a touch furtive about him," I said. "What do you expect?" he replied. "He's a Corsican." He was death—and always amusing—on pretension. I once told him about a Czech we both knew who, thinking to establish his family's *haute bourgeois* standing, told me that, in Prague, his father never shaved himself, but had a barber come in each morning to shave him. My friend paused, then said, "You know, Joseph, the truth is that his father probably shaved his mother."

In the twenty-three years of our friendship—and over that time I saw him regularly—he never repeated himself. I had seen him in a wide variety of company—from clerks to clerics to eminences of various kinds—and he was able to get on easily with them all, without changing his manner and yet never seeming to condescend nor wishing to establish his superiority. With his impressively wide outlook, his deep culture, he reminded me by his person of the importance of keeping a high standard. He enlarged my view of the world; he never allowed me to forget that, for people on whom nothing is missed, it was a place of unending interest.

He manipulated language marvelously. I once described an acquaintance we had in common as "rat-faced." "Yes," he said, "you are correct: He is quite rodential." Rodential—it sounds like nothing so much as an insurance company for mice. He had an extensive Yiddish vocabulary, which he wielded chiefly to humorous effect. He read German and French, but in an elaborate metaphor described his knowledge of the latter as resembling the condition of a cabinet filled with delicate glassware in a home hit by a bomb during the German blitz: "Shards, only shards, remain."

Not a few people described him as curmudgeonly. He was not ill-tempered but tact, especially in the presence of what he might have called "educated ignorance," was not his primary interest. He once told me that at a dinner party a woman expressed extravagant admiration for the novels of Philip Roth. "Even though married, then," he said when she had finished, "I take it that, like Roth, you approve of adultery." Imagine please what this did to the remainder of that evening's dinner-table conversation. "Funny," he said after recounting this to me, "but I seem to get invited out less and less."

One of his graduate students told me that, in a paper he had written for him, he described a work of social science as "an orgy of insight." Going over the paper with him, my friend said he wondered if his student had really thought much about what an orgy might be like. "Consider the bodies, some less than shapely, a few possibly even grotesque, the smells, the sounds. Having done so, I think you may wish to find a better word than *orgy*."

When I was in his company, I felt myself to be wittier. The world seemed a more amusing place. No one who met him ever seems to have forgot him, for the force of his personality left an indelible impress. He lavished the gift of his charm on me and on a small band of friends and promising students. Even today, more than twenty years after his death, when I come upon an odd scene, or read about outrageous behavior on the part of an academic or intellectual, I wish he were still about so that he could bestow his invariably witty and penetrating comment on the matter. His friendship changed my life, making it richer, happier, more exhilarating.

Is it possible that the young, those still under thirty, are unaware of the existence of charm, having grown up without many available models of the charming to consider? Is charm for them found in the rebarbatively abrasiveness of comedians making jokes on Comedy Central about fellatio, menstrual cycles, and masturbation? Can they possibly discover charm in rappers telling us what racist swine we all—but them—are? Or in our current late-night talk-show hosts scoring cheap political points, with smirks added? Has the culture in which they have come to live deadened them to the possibilities of charm? If there are charmless ages, might they, and we with them, be living in one currently?

Those of us who have at various times been under the spell of charm know that without it something is missing from life. What is missing is the prospect of virtuosity of personality, of witnessing or (better) being in the company of people imbued with a magical quality that brings pleasure to others. The absence of charm is a substantial substraction from the roster of life's pleasures.

Provoke delight, arouse approval, display a good heart, never produce tedium or satiety, continually give pleasure, be the person others want never to leave the room, however you define charm, while in its presence, there is no mistaking its wondrous enlivening quality. Even at the second remove of movies or television, at concerts or in recorded music, charm, when it turns up, lends life luster. Charm widens the lens, heightens the color of life, intensifies and sweetens it. Charm is one of life's luxuries. We can, of course, all live without it. What a great pity, though, to do so!

INDEX

About the Author

Joseph Epstein was the editor of the *American Scholar* between 1974 and 1997 and taught in the English Department at Northwestern University between 1973 and 2002. His essays and short stories have appeared in the *New Yorker*, the *Atlantic*, *Harper's*, *Commentary*, the *Weekly Standard*, and the *London Times Literary Supplement*. He was awarded a National Humanities Medal in 2003.